D1592856

Photograph of P. I. Tchaikovsky, signed and inscribed to Gustave Schirmer, founder of the house

The QUEEN OF SPADES

An Opera in Three Acts and Seven Scenes

by

PETER ILYITCH TCHAIKOVSKY

Libretto by

MODESTE TCHAIKOVSKY

English Version by

ROSA NEWMARCH

G. SCHIRMER *New York/London*

Characters.

Herman	*1-st Tenor.*	Lisa	*Soprano.*
Count Tomsky (Plutus)	*Baritone.*	Pauline (Daphnis)	*Contralto.*
Prince Yeletsky	*Baritone.*	The Governess	*Mezzo-Soprano.*
Tchekalinsky	*Tenor.*	Mary	*Soprano.*
Sourin	*Bass.*		
Tchaplitsky	*2-nd Tenor.*		
Naroumov	*2-nd Bass.*		
Master of the Ceremonies	*2-nd Tenor.*		
Countess ***	*Mezzo-Soprano.*		

Characters in the Interlude.

a) Chloë	*Soprano.*
b) Daphnis (Pauline)	*Contralto.*
c) Plutus (Count Tomsky)	*Baritone.*

The scene is laid in St. Petersburg at the close of the Eighteenth Century.

Index to Contents.

The Queen of Spades

English version by Rosa Newmarch
(after the Russian of Modeste Tchaikovsky)

Peter Ilyitch Tchaikovsky, Op. 68

INTRODUCTION.

Printed in the U. S. A.

pesante e marcato
cresc.

molto espr.
mf
p
po - - co a
po - co cresc.
f
ff
Timp.
poco dim.
mf
p
pp

ACT I.

SCENE I.

Spring. A open space in the Summer Garden, St. Petersburg. Seated on the benches are nurses and governesses, chatting together. Some of the children are playing at races; others have skipping-ropes, balls etc.

№1. Chorus of Children, Nurses etc.

cre - - scen - -
- do
c. t. c.
Voices of little girls.
Mousie, while you're a - ble, Run beneath the ta - ble,

(Sounds of laughter, exclamations, and running footsteps.)
Who'll catch me!
cre - scen - do
mf
CHORUS.
Alti. NURSE-MAIDS.
f
Gai - ly laugh and play, Child - ren, while you may! Now's the time for sport,
p
North - ern springs are short, Sun - shine will not stay!
mf
Child-ren, when you're good, Nei - ther cross nor rude, In your games a - gree,
p

play - ing pret-ti-ly, Then we nurs-es too, get some rest from you,
p cre - scen - -
Thank - ful for the chance, While you run and dance. Gai - ly laugh and play,
- - do
ff
mf
Child - ren, while you may, Now's the time for sport, North - ern springs are short!
p
CHORUS OF GOVERNESSES.
Sop.
f
Heav'n be prais'd, for now a while our end-less du-ties cease! Here we sit & breathe the balm-y
Child ren!
mf

air of spring in peace! Dai - ly scoldings, marks and lessons, Cop - y - books and slates—
while you may, Gai - ly laugh and play, Now's the
p
Rest - ing in this sunny garden, We for - get our fates!
time for sport, North - ern springs are short!
CHORUS OF HEAD NURSES.
Sopr.
mf Hush - a - hush - a -
Alti.
p
bye! Hush - a - hush - a - bye!
mf Hush - a - hush - a - bye! Hush - a - hush - a -
Hush, my ba - by, from the light, Keep those pret - ty
bye! Hush, ba - by,

eyes shut tight.
(Children's drums and trumpets are heard off the stage.)
(Children's drums & trumpets.)
Trumpets.
ff
cre - scen - do
f
Sop.
CHORUS OF NURSES & GOVERNESSES.
mf
Here come our gallant soldier boys, they march so straight,
Alti.
Toy trumpets.
Drums.
p
so stead - y!
Now stand a - side there!
Now stand a - side there!
Now stand a - side there!

Make way! make way!
One, two, right, left,
One, two, right, left!
(Enter the boys playing at soldiers, led by their captain.)
più f
p
CHOR. OF BOYS (marching).
ff
One, two, one, two,
right, left, right, left,
Keep in step, boys! All to - gether!
BOY CAPTAIN. Right wheel! One! two! Halt! (The boys come to a stand still.)
BOY CAPTAIN. Attention! Shoulder arms! Present arms! Ground arms! (The boys carry out the orders.)
mf
p 3
(Tromba)

CHOR. OF BOYS.
Now 'gainst our country's foe we're marching with our banners, We mean to let them know That
Sostenuto, ma lo stesso tempo.
we'll soon teach them manners, and win the day or die! Hurrah! Hurrah! Hurrah!
cresc.
For hearth and home we fight, To save the land we cherish,
Fl.
etc.
We'll put the foe to flight, or 'neath their swords will perish, for we must win or die! Hurrah!
cresc.
Hurrah! Hurrah!
Long life to thee, our queen, Our

mo_ther, wise and glor_ious, Our em_press most serene, Till we return vic_tor_ious, To
greet our land a_gain! Hur_rah! Hur_rah! Hur_rah!
ff
f
BOY CAPTAIN. „Ready, my lads?"
BOY SOLDIERS. At your orders, Captain!
BOY CAPTAIN. Attention! Present arms! Shoulder arms! Trail arms! Right wheel! March!
Toy drums.
ff
Toy trumpets.
ff
sfp
sf
fp
sf
mf
(Exit boys with drums & trumpets.)
mf
Come prima.
Sop.
CHORUS OF NURSES AND GOVERNESSES.
Alti.
See, how our brave & youthful sol_diers can march as straight and
Come prima.
po_co a po_co dim.

gal - lantly as men!
Brave sol-dier boys,
march on - ward,
p
pp
brave soldier
boys!
brave soldier boys!
(Exeunt. The other children also follow the boy-soldiers. The Nurses and Governesses disperse, making room for other promenaders.)
p
pp
pp
Alto.
Cor.
Cl.
ppp
(Enter Tchekalins. & Sourin.)

№ 2. Scene Arioso: Herman.

Moderato.
Recit.
TCHEKALINSKY.
What luck had you last night at cards?
Recit.
SOURIN.
Of course, I lost no end of mon - ey!
Moderato.
PIANO.
p
TCHEK.
SOUR.
S.
I have no luck. You kept it up, no doubt, till day - light? Yes, before t'was over,
p
mf
how bored I was! Dev - il take it, I was quite clear'd out!
TCHEK:
SOUR.
Was Herman there? Yes! He
p
f
in tempo
sat as us - ual there, the whole night long; till dawn, One might suppose they nail'd him to the boards, and
p
TCHEK.
SOUR.
TCHEK.
drank, but ne - ver spoke a word. Was that all? He watch'd how oth - er people played. Ah,
mf

SOUR.
T.
what a cur_ious man he is! As though he had an e_vil con_science, op_press'd by
TCHEK.
SOUR.
Andte (♩=72)
S.
man_y past mis_deeds. I've heard it said, he has no money. True, he is poor.
Andante.
mf
p espr.
(Enter Herman, dreamy and melancholy, together with Count Tomsky.)
(Exit Sourin and Tchek.)
S.
See, there he comes! He looks like some lost soul, so ghast_ly.
Ob.
più f
p
Ob.
HERMAN.
Why, no_thing, all is well...
TOMSKY.
Come, tell me, Her_man, what's the matter? What ails you?
p

H.
No-thing at all.
T.
But you have alt-er'd, Her-man, now, you seem un-happy.
T.
You were a care-ful, steady lad, but chee-ry too, and full of
T.
spir-its; but now you're gloom-y, tac-it-turn,— and I can scarce be-
T.
lieve mine ears; 'tis said your passion's all for cards; that all the night you sit and play, till sun-rise

Andante. (♩= 72)
HERMAN.
T.
finds you at the tables. True! Now no long - er can I
Andante.
p
H.
tread life's beat-en path-ways as in the past. I know not what has come to me.
3
p
più f
H.
Con-scious of ru - in, and re-sent-ing my weakness, yet I lack the power to check my down-fall.
p
TOMSKY.
H.
I am in love, in love! What! you in love? With
mf
HERMAN. dolce
T.
whom? I have not learnt her name or sta - tion. Nor sought to
p
p

H.
più f
make her mine. She needs no mort_al ap_pel_la_tion who is di_
p
p
p
(with ardour) Più mosso.
vine... With what bright thing may I com_
string.
Più mosso.
p
pare her? This earth no im_age yields, since
Par_a_dise holds no_thing rar_er in all th'El_ys_sian
p
poco cresc.
fields! Yet hate_ful thoughts pur_sue me: what if an_
riten.
f
a tempo sempre agitato
rit.
mf
a tempo sempre agitato

H.
o - - ther owns her heart, while I scarce dare to kiss her
p
p
foot - prints, and, torn with pain, must stand a - part...
riten.
Tempo I. (Andante.)
I curse myself, but love en -
mf
dim.
p
thralls me; I strive in vain in pas - sion's grasp, and long the more her form to clasp,
Riten. molto.
string.
f
ff
più f
Tempo I.
a piàcere
and long the more her form to clasp; I strive in vain in passion's grasp, and long the more her
colla parte
mf
p

riten.
Adagio.
H.
form to clasp! I have not learnt her name or sta - tion, Nor sought to make her
riten.
Adagio.
H
mine!
TOMSKY. Allegro non troppo. (♩ = 108)
If things are so, my friend, you'd
Allegro non troppo.
T
better make haste to learn her name, then start to woo by signal and by let-ter and boldly claim her
HERMAN.
T.
heart... Ah no, a-las! Too high her state, to me she never will be grant-ed!
H.
TOMSKY.
These are the fears by which I'm haunted! Well, there are oth-ers, girls to pick and choose from.
riten.
riten.

HERMAN
Poco più vivo. (♩= 116)
Ah! you know me lit - tle! My love for her will never
Poco più vivo.
Cl.
cease! Nay, Tom - sky! Vows are not so brit - tle!
Once I knew hap - pi - ness and peace, in days e'er passion had possess'd me, my
Fl.
spi - rit was by reas - on led, But since this ard - ent dream ob - sess'd me With
vis ions strange, my rest has fled, my rest has
cre
scen do

H.
fled! Like poi - son all my veins it fills! I languish! Mine the
mf
cresc.
f
H.
love that kills! What's all this, Her-man? I con - fess, I never
TOMSKY.
ff
p
T.
thought, that you of all men could be by passion so dis -
cre - - scen - do
(Exit Herman & Tomsky. The stage is filled with promenaders.)
T.
traught!
poco stringendo
ff

№ 3. Chorus of Promenaders. Scene.

Allegro giusto. (♩ = 126)
Sop.
Alt.
Tenor.
Bass.
GENERAL CHORUS OF PROMENADERS.
Now, thank Heav'n, no more it freez - es, Win - ter's o - ver.
Allegro giusto.
PIANO.
past! Bright the skies and warm the breez - es, May is here at
last! Ah! 't is too en - chanting, these are days for out - door

bliss!
Pleasure's har_vest, let us reap it,
Who can say how long we
keep it, Weath _ er such as this?
Who can
say how long we keep it, who can say,
Weather such as this?
ff
p

(Young ladies.)
How delight_ful! How enchanting!
(Old ladies.)
Sure_ly life was bright - - er, in the years long past,
(Young beaux.)
Sun_ny skies, sweet breezes, Song of night_in_gale,
(Old beaux.)
Ma_ny years have van - - ish'd since on such a day,
Ah, we feel that life is sweet!
Then the spring was ear_lier, sun_ny days would last. Aye, spring was always earl - y!
love_ly girls, whose blush - - es make the ros_es pale.
we went forth a - court - - ing in the month of May.

'Tis de_light_ful in the park to meet!
Now bright days grow rar - - er, summer's of_ten cold,
Springtide stirs our fan_cies, love-dreams haunt our sleep.
Gai_et_y seems ban - - ish'd, changed our ways and climes.
Yes, we feel the Sum - mer— Garden makes life sweet!
nothing seems im - prov - - ing now we're get - ting old!
and sweet ex_pect - a - - tions make our pul - - ses
ev' ry_thing was bet - - ter in the good old times, old
cresc.
mf
f
p

Yes, we see with sat_is _ fac_tion hosts of suitors, young and gay,
Yes, we're sure that things were brighter, men po _ li _ ter, balls more gay,
leap!
Sun_ny skies, soft breezes, ten_der songs of the
times!
Ma_ny, ma_ny years have vanish'd since on such a
Timp.
Of_fi_cers and smart civ _ il_ians crowd the gar_den paths to_day.
Love was tru_er, skies were blu_er, and less rare a sun _ _ ny day!
night - in_gale,
love_ly girls whose blushes make the summer ros_es
per . fect day.
We went out a_cour_ting, cour_ting in the hap_py

cre_ _scen_ _do
Look how man _ y well_dress'd peo _ ple in the gar _ dens take their air _ ing!
Yes, we're sure that life was bright _ er, men po_li _ ter, balls more splen _ did,
seem quite pale, These are spring times ra _ diant of_f'rings, These the gifts of
month of May! Gai _ e_ty is ban _ ish'd, changed our cust _ oms and our
pp po _ co a po _ co cre_ _scen_
Gallant sold _ iers, smart civ_il _ ians, What fine clothes and noble bear _ ing!
clouds were few _ er, skies were blu _ er, all was bet _ ter, all was bet _ ter,
May! Aye, these are spring _ tides' radiant of _ f'rings, gifts of May. Now spring is
climes. Yes, ev' ry _ thing was bet_ter, sure _ ly in old times, Yes ev' ry _
_ _ do
mf

ff
See, what crowds of welldress'd people take their airing!
all was bet_ter in the good old days now ended!
come and brings us gladness love and endless pleasure!
thing was bet_ter in the good old days now vanish'd!
f
Now, thank Heav'n, no
more it freez_es, Win_ter's o_ver_past!
Bright the skies and
warm the breez_es, May is here at last!
Ah! 't is too en_chanting, these are

days of out-door bliss!
Pleasure's harv-est, let us reap it,
Who can say, how long we keep it, Weath - er such as this? Who can
ff
ff
ff
ff
ff
(Enter Herman & Tomsky.)
Poco meno. (♩ = 112)
TOMSKY
And are you
say how long we keep it? Who can say? Weather such as this!
Poco meno.
p
p

T.
certain she ignores your love and your existence? I'll dare to
p
T.
bet she sighs for you, and loves you at a distance...
Moderato. (♩ = 100)
HERMAN.
con amarezza
Ah, had I not this consolation to ease my pain,
Moderato.
Cor.
H.
I think my heart with desolation would break in twain!

poco riten.
H
Al_though I live thro' an_guish wear_ing, there's still one thought be_
colla parte
a tempo
H
yond all bear_ing: Should fate de_cree she ne'er shall be my bride...
a tempo
cre_ scen_
H.
TOM. HERMAN.
Ah, then for me remains one end... What? Su_i_
do
f p
animando (Enter Prince Yeletsky. Tchekalinsky and Tomsky approach him.)
TCHEK. (to the Prince)
H.
cide! I wish you
espressivo
p
cre_ scen_
SOURIN. THE PRINCE. (riten.)
H
all good luck. They say you are en_gaged? Yes, gentle_men, it
do
mf

Meno mosso. (♩ = 84)
P
is so; she's an an_gel, and whisper'd „Yes" this morning, So we're plight_ed henceforth
Meno mosso.
p
P
for ever mo re! Good news, in_deed! Take my con_grat_u_la_tions, all
Più vivo. (♩ = 104)
TCHEK.
SOUR.
Più vivo.
mf
f
TOM.
THE PRINCE.
riten.
S.
hap_pi_ness! Yel_et_sky, my good wishes! I thank you all, dear friends!
mf
Andante. (♩ = 76)
HERM.
(with feeling)
O day of an_guish, be ác_curst for ev - - er!
P
O day of bliss and hopes ful_fill'd, be blest for
Andante.
p
f

H.
mf
In which all mi_series un_i_ted combine to ru_in life's endeav_our.
P.
mf
più f
ev _ er! In which all joys un _ i _ ted com_bine to crown my
p
p
più f
H.
My, dear _ est hopes are crush'd & blighted; Some hearts may feast, but mine must fast.
T. P.
life's en_deav _ _ our, Henceforth my years are light _ ed with rays direct from
più f
f
H.
All na_ture frowns on me, such sad _ ness floods all my soul and dims mine eyes; My
f
P.
heaven cast... All na_ture smiles on me; such gladness floods all my
mf
p

H.
poison'd thoughts drive me to madness, my poi - son'd thoughts drive me to madness,
P.
heart and blinds mine eyes; There is no room for doubt or sad - ness, Now love has
f
p
H.
yet great - er torments I surmise! O day of grief and an - guish, Ac-
P.
op - en'd Par - a - dise! O, day of per - fect bliss, be blest by me while
Poco più. (♩= 88)
H.
curst while life shall last! No, tell us all a - bout her!
TOM.
P.
life shall last! But, Prince, you have not told her name? (Enter Lisa and the Countess.)
Poco più.
p
mf
p
p
mar -

THE PRINCE. (pointing out Lisa.)
HERM.
Here she comes!
My love!
my love!
whom he has
crescendo
f
-cato in la mano sinistra
H.
chos - en!
O
heav - en!
This un -
f
LISA AND THE COUNTESS.
TOM.
H.
does me!
'T is
he
a - gain!
Is
this
di - mi - nu - en - do
T.
your nameless la - dy - love?
The beau - ty
you a -
p

№ 4. Quintetto & Scene.

Andante. (♩ = 60)
LISA.
I shud_der! Once a_gain he re_ap pears,
COUNTESS.
I shud_der! Wan and sad he re_ap_pears,
HERMAN.
I shud_der! Dark & threat_ning she ap_pears a
TOMSKY.
dor'd? She, his one de sir'd
THE PRINCE.
I shud_der! Wan & strange she now ap_pears,
Andante.
PIANO.
L.
This gloom_y man, this most mys_terious stranger! He trou_bles me with
C.
This gloom_y man, this most mys_terious stranger! O, fate_ful ap_par_
H.
gain, like some strange har_bing_er of ill, this weird old wom_an. Her looks of condem_
T.
mate, The Prin_ce's bride! Ah, cru_el fate!
P.
What cause has she to look so pale & so af_fright_ed? dis_tract_ed and ex_

L.
name_less fears, On me his dumb, re_proach_ful glan_ces
C.
i_tion! Who is he, on me threat'ning
H.
na - - - - tion op_press and fill my heart with
T.
I now see ter_ror in his eyes, ter - - ror in his
P.
ci - - - - ted? She seems possess'd by sud_den, name_less
mp
f
L.
turn_ing... Who thus pur_sues me wheresoe'er I go? I
C.
glan_ces turn_ing? Who thus pur_sues me where_so e'er I go?
H.
nameless fears! Why does she want to dog my foot_steps, whereso_e'er I go?
T.
eyes, That were with pas_sion flam - ing!
P.
fears! O, must our bliss, but new_ly found, so soon by grief be
mf
f

L.
C.
H.
T.
P.
f
mf
fear him! Fear his eye with mad - ness
What can he want, this unknown man? I
I quail be - neath the glance she turns on me,—
And what ails her? She looks so pale and
blight - - ed? What cloud has come be-tween us
burn - ing, His wild un - can - ny look, that haunts me
fear his eye with mad - ness burning, His wild un-can-ny look that haunts me
She saps my will & strength, Who can she
white? strange and white! Ah, my heart misgives me
now? I shud-der, what dis - ast - - er then is

L.
C.
H.
T.
P.
riten.
so! I shud_der! I shud_der, 'neath his
so! I shud_der! I shud_der, 'neath his
be? I shud_der! I shud_der, 'neath her
quite! I shud_der! I shud_der, 'neath her
dim.
this, that comes be_tweenme and my new_found bliss? I shud_der 'neath her
Allegro non tanto. (♩ = 116)
gaze!
gaze!
gaze!
(Count Tomsky approaches the Countess. The Prince goes towards Lisa. The Countess stares fixedly at Herman.)
gaze! Well, Count_ess!
gaze!
Allegro non tanto.

COUNTESS.
T.
My warm con.grat_u _ la_tions...
O, tell me, quick,
poco cresc.
TOM.
C.
that of_fi_cer, who is he?
Yes, which one?
That one?
p
COUNTESS.
T.
Her_man, a friend of mine.
He looks so pale and strange.
mf
(Tomsky and the Countess pass to the back of the stage.)
C.
Where does he come from?
p marcato
mf

Moderato assai. (♩ = 96)
THE PRINCE (offering his hand to Lisa).
The rad_iant skies, the sunny hours, The spring with all her train of flow'rs
Moderato assai.
dolce
p
mf
p
P.
This crowd of kindly friends who meet to bless, and wish us ev'ry hap_pi_ness in
riten.
riten.
mf
p
P.
HERMAN (menacingly).
fu_ture... (they pass) Laugh a_way, my friend, for_get_ful that the temp_est fol_lows
p
(Distant thunder. Herman sinks down on the bench in gloomy reverie.)
H.
sunny weather; and that our Mak_er turns joy to weeping; sends bolts from the blue!
cresc.
p
f
p

№ 5. Scene and Ballad (Tomsky)

Andante. (♩ = 72)
SOURIN.
A queer old creat_ure this an_cient
Andante.
espr.
mf
PIANO.
TCHEKALINSKY.
TOMSKY
S.
Count_ess! A scare _ crow! No won_der she is al_ways called the
T.
Queen of Spades! There's one thing puzzles me: now she
p
SOURIN.
nev_er plays at cards as formerly. What? That old thing played?

TCHEK.
TOM.
That weird old mummy gambling half the night! (ha ha ha) Why, sure_ly you must have heard
S.
You're jok_ing!
mf
f
T.
SOUR.
TCHEK.
stor_ies a_bout her? No, never, not a word! Not a word!
TOM.
riten.
Adagio. (♩ = 60)
Well then I'll tell the tale! The Countess years a_go was known in Paris as belle of all the
balls; while all the gay and smart young men pursued her. They nicknamed her the Ve - nus of Mos_cow.
Count Saint-Germain, so gossip ran, (in those days he was handsome) was head & ears in love and tried in

T.
vain to cap - ti - vate the Countess! For ev' ry ev'ning found her deep in-volved in Fa - ro.
p
cre - scen - do
T
A las! She much pre-ferr'd the cards to Love.
mf
p
Allegro con spirito. (♩ = 116)
T.
It chanced at Versail - les „au jeu de la Reine; „The" Mos - covite Ve-nus" had
Allegro con spirito.
p
p
T.
lost her last sou, And near her at ta - ble was Count Saint-Germain,*) Who
riten.
T.
watch'd her ill - for - tune the whole ev' - ning through. She mut - ter'd with fur - ious re -
riten.

 *) Pronounce Germaine

Quasi andante.
T.
gards: How fool - ish, how fool - ish, How
Quasi andante.
mf
f
p
f
p
Tempo I.
T.
fool - ish, to ven - ture my mon - ey so fast, For now I be - lieve that my
Tempo I.
pp
poco
a
poco
cresc.
a piacere
in tempo.
T.
luck's turn'd at last! Three cards, o, three cards, o, three cards!
in tempo.
mf
ff
T.
The Count takes the mo - ment, a - wait - ed so long, And
p
T.
when his a - dor'd one has slipped from the room, He fol - lows, and finds her a -
m.d.

T.
part from the throng, Re-gret-ting her los-ses in si-lence and gloom. No
riten.
riten.
Quasi andante.
longer his suit he re-tards. „Dear Count-ess, dear Count-ess, dear
Quasi andante.
mf
f p
f p
Tempo I.
Count-ess, oh grant me but one „ren-dez-vous," And then, if you wish, I will
Tempo I
pp cre scen do
a piacere
name them to you three cards, yes, three cards, yes, three
mf
in tempo.
cards!" The Count-ess, in-dig-nant, cries:
in tempo.
ff
mf
f

T.
„Sir, do you dare!" The Count stands his ground... E're the sun rose a-
Tromba.
mf
gain the la-dy was back at the tab-les, I'll swear; though emp-ty her
pp
poco a poco cresc
pockets for „jeu de la Reine," she'd mast-er'd the names of three cards...
f
Meno mosso.
She raked in the mo-ney, the oth-ers all lost,
Meno mosso.
f
riten.
She piled up her gains.— Did she think of the cost of three cards, three cards, three
riten.
Andante.
p
Andante.
p

Tempo I.
T.
cards?
She
Tempo I.
once named three cards to her hus - band, t'was said; And
whis - per'd them once to a gal - lant young spark, But
while that same night she lay qui - et in bed, A
ghost stood be - fore her and spoke in the
cre - - - scen - - - do

T.
dark... „Death's warn - - ing no wight dis - re -
mf p cre - - scen - -
gards; Thou shalt die when a third man, im - pell'd by despair, shall
f
do f p cre - - scen - -
strive from thy bos - om the se - - - cret to tear of three cards,
ff a
do f
piacere
of three cards, of three cards!
Poco più mosso.
Three cards!"
ff
ff

№ 6. Closing scene (storm).

T.
and pond - er it!
„When a third man, im - pell'd by his
S.
„When a third man, im - pell'd by his
pp
marcato
T.
love and des - pair shall strive from thy bos - om the
S.
love and des - pair shall strive from thy bos om the
T.
se - - - cret to tear of three cards,
S.
se - - - cret to tear of three cards,
mf
f
f
T.
of three cards, of three cards!"
(exeunt Tchekalinsky & Sourin.)
S.
of three cards, of three cards!"

(A loud clap of thunder. The storm bursts overhead and the promenaders are seen hurrying in all directions.)

How quick - ly the stormclouds have gath'er'd! Why, who could have thought!
gather'd! Why,who could have thought such rain was com - ing!
hark!
who could have thought such rain, such rain was com - ing!
p
the light - ning is flash - ing, thun - der is roll - ing!
the light - ning is flash - ing, thun der is roll - ing!
cre - scen - do
fff
Make haste to get home!
fff
fff
Make haste to get home!
fff
8
fff
fff

Now run
for
the
gates
e're
we're drenched!
Now
(All hurry off. The thunder gets louder.)
(voices dying away.)
Come
(distant.)
Come, hast - en home!
run
for
the
gates!
(distant.)
Come, hast - en home!
f
mf
hast - en home!
How
wet
we
are!
Now, run
for
the
(distant.)
Come home!
(distant)
Now run
for
the
gates!
Come home!
Now run
for
the
gates!
espr.
p

gates!
Be_fore
our frocks are quite
spoilt!
Make
Make haste!
Be_fore
your frocks are quite spoilt!
Make haste!
Make haste!
cre
scen
haste!
(A loud clap of thunder.)
do
fff
ff
dim.
HERMAN. (in a reverie)
„Death's warn - ing no wight dis - re
m.d.
pp
cre
scen
marcato

H.
gards:
Thou shalt
die when a third man, im-pell'd by des-pair, shall
strive from thy bos - om the se - cret to tear of three
cards, of three cards, of three cards!"
What use to me
would be this luck - y com - bin - a - tion? Since
m. d.
pp
cresc.
ff
p
f
espress.
Cel.

H.
all my hopes are fled? An-other calls her bride!
cre - scen - do
ff
Cor.
The storm can-not fright me! My
mf
in-most soul is riv - en with such des-pair and grief, such
wild re-venge-ful pas-sions, the tempest seems as nought beside them!
И. Т. Д.
No, Prince! While I have

H.
breath, I will not give her up to you! She shall be mine, I know not
mf
mf
H.
how!
cresc.
fff
H.
ff
Wind, lightning,
ff
H.
thun - - - der! I call to
p
p
ff
p
H.
wit - - ness here my solemn oath:
f
p
p
ff
p

H
She ne'er shall be an - oth er's,
she shall be mine, I swear it,
my own
in life or in death!
(Herman hastens away.
Curtain.)
p
f
ff
8

End of First Scene.

SCENE II.

Lisa's room. A door opening on to the balcony which leads into the garden.

№ 7. Duet.

Andantino mosso. (♩ = 80)
LISA.
(Lisa is seated at a harpsichord, Pauline and her girl friends are grouped around her.)
PAULINE.
Andantino mosso.
Fl.
PIANO.
p
tr
L.
p
1. Al - read - y, shades of night the dis - tant fields en - fold; From
2. Si - lent lies the gar - den, wrapp'd as in a dream; While
P.
p
pp
pp
L.
yon - der tower the last bright shafts of day have fad - ed; The
far a - way, be - tween the ranks of weep - ing wil - lows, My
P.
p
p

L.
run ning brook re _ flects one gleam of sun _ set gold; Now day de _ parts
ear can catch the whis _ per'd se _ cret of the stream, Sung low by ti _
P.
by gloom in _ vad _ ed, gloom in _ vad _ _ ed.
ny crystal bil _ lows, crystal bil _ _ lows.
LISA.
1.
2.
How How sweet to breathe the warm &
PAULINE.

L.
per - fume laden breeze, How clear and mu - sic - al the ripple of the
P.
p
L.
ri - ver, How soft - ly moves the wind a -
P.
p
L.
mong the slumb'ring trees, the weeping wil - - lows wake and
P.
f
mf
L.
shiv - er, wake and shiv - er.
P.
tr
p

№ 8. Scene Pauline's Romance and Russian song with chorus.

O please, mesdames, just one more
LISA.
PAULINE.
Paul_ine, dear, now sing a _ lone! A _ lone! What can I sing?
song!
Sing what you please, Paul
P.
Well then I'll sing you Lis_
riten.
ine, dear, but be a dar_ling, sing us just one song!
riten.

 39106

(Pauline seats herself at the harpsichord.)
P.
a's fav_or_ite song.
Let's see now...
How it goes...
p
Andante non tanto. (♩ = 76)
Andante non tanto.
(Pauline preluding.)
mf
10
13
13
17
10
12
11
Ah! now I know
(with deep sentiment)
Dear friends for whom I sing, dear friends for

P.
whom I sing, Who know nor care nor sor - row, But still can
più f
dim.
P.
sport in hap - py groves and sun - ny fields. I
p
P.
too once dwelt a - mong the peace - ful groves of
P.
f
Ar - ca - die, Have hail'd the dawn of joy ful days up - on this
più f
P
self - same earth, And known the bliss of liv - ing, and known the
mf
p

P.
bliss, the bliss of liv - - - - ing. The
p
gold - - en dreams of love, my earl - ier years have
cresc.
bright - en'd, — A - las! of all those fair and ra - diant vi - sions Now re -
poco cresc.
ff
mains one hope a - lone, one hope re - mains a - lone: Death
mf
calls me, Death calls me, Death calls - - -
dim.

P.
me!
(All are deeply touched by the song.)
Recit.
Now, what could I be think_ing of
to sing this tearful dit_ty? Ah, how thoughtless! A_part from that you
in tempo
have some troub_le, Lis - a. But what in_deed can vex you, on your be_
in tempo
Recit.
(the girls)
tro_thal day! Dear, dear, dear! Now ev - ry bo_dy seems in dole_ful dumps!

P.
in tempo
Let's tune up something lively,
A Russ - ian air, a bri - dal
Cl. in tempo
mf
folk-song!
I'll start it, girls,
ad libitum.
and you must sing the
Poco meno. (♩ = 69)
chorus!
CHORUS.
Sop.
Yes, that's right!
A Russ - ian song,
Alti.
mf
Yes, that's right!
Poco meno.
Allegro. (♩ = ♪ del precedente)
PAULINE.
Now, my dar - ling, now, Ma - ry,
A mer - ry Russ - ian song!
The girls clap with their hands.
(Lisa takes ho part in the merriment, but stands lost in trought on the balcony.)
p
73

P.
Come be gay, dance a d play! Hey, fol-de - rol de-did-dle, Come be gay, dance and play!
f
Hey, fol-de - rol de-did-dle, Come be gay, dance and play!
etc.
f
P.
Clap your hands so white, Ma-ry, on your hips, on your hips, Hey, fol-de-rol de-diddle!
Hey, fol-de-rol de-diddle!
mp
mf
P.
Clap your hands on your hips, While each nim-ble foot, Ma-ry, gai-ly trips,
Clap your hands on your hips,
mf

P.
gai_ly trips! Hey, fol_de_rol de_did_dle, with_out slips, gai_ly trips!
Hey, fol_de_rol de_did_dle, with_out slips, gai_ly trips!
tr
f
P.
ff
Should your mo_ther scold, Ma_ry, ne_ver cry, just re_ply! Hey, fol_de_rol de_did_dle:
(Pauline and some of the girls begin dance.)
ff
Hey, fol_de_rol de_did_dle:
ff
mf
P.
I'll be wise, by and by! Should your Dad be cross, Ma_ry, Don't give way, Laugh and say,
I'll be wise, by and by!
mf

P.
Hey, fol_de_rol de_did_dle! „I'll be gay, While I may!“ Should your sweet_heart
Hey, fol_de_rol de_did_dle! „I'll be gay, While I may!“
P.
frown, Ma_ry, Say „good bye, go your way!“ Hey, fol_de_
Hey, fol_de_
P.
rol de_did_dle, Say „goodbye, go your way!“
rol de_did_dle, Say „good_bye go your way!“

№ 9. Scene and Arioso (The Governess.)

G.
Ev_en when alone to_geth_er
act as though en eviden_ce.
p
mf
p
G.
On_ly at some rus_tic wed_ding
mf
G.
You might dance like that,
mes mignonnes!
p
p
G.
Here, dear girls, you must re_mem_ber
ne_ver to out -
mf
p
p
G.
rage bon_ton! *)
Here, dear girls, you must re_mem_ber
mf

*) Pronounce *tonne* to rhyme with mignonnes.

G.
ne_ver to outrage *bon - ton!*
La_dies born to grace high circles must mind the *con_venances,*
and ev_en when a_lone to_gether act as though
en év - i - dence! act as though
en év - i - dence!
mf
p
f

№ 10. Closing scene.

L'istesso tempo.
THE GOVERNESS.
'T is time you all went home. I was sent to bid you put on your
L'istesso tempo.
PIANO.
mf
tr
(The young ladies disperse.)
PAULINE. (approaching Lisa)
L.
cloaks.
Lis_a, tell me,
p
LISA.
G.
why are you so gloomy?
I? nonsense, dear! what fan_cies!
Now look how calm &
PAUL.
P.
fair the world ap_pears at twi_light;
see, af_ter storm what peace.
Take

Allegro moderato. (♩ = 120)
P.
care, lest I should tell the Prince that you were weeping and ve-ry glum up - on the
Allegro moderato.
p
mf
day of your be - troth - al...
LISA.
No! I im-plore you,
f
mf
f
L.
say not a word!
PAULINE.
Then let me see you smile, dear.
mf
dim.
p
p
p
Come, look hap - py! That's right! And now good -
mf
mf
(They kiss.)
LISA.
(Exeunt.)
bye!
Wait, I will come, Paul-ine...
p
p
pp

Andante. (♩ = 66)
(Enter a servant who extinguishes all the lights, leaving only one candle.
As she is about to close the door of the balcony, Lisa returns.)
C.I.
p
cre
scen
do
f
LISA.
Stay, do not shut the door, 't is
close.
No, Mary, nights now are warm; warm and so still!
MARY.
Will not my lady soon feel chilly?
p
MARY.
My lady does not need me now?
LISA.
No, many thanks, now
Cl.
go to bed.
pp
MARY.
Dear lady it grows late...
LISA.
Well, leave me. Good-
cre
scen
do

(Exit Mary. Lisa stands as though lost in thought, and then begins to weep quietly.)
L.
night!
p
f
pp
(with much sentiment.)
O burn_ing tears of girl _ hood, why must ye flow?
A _ las, youth's radiant visions, Ah, say, why must ye go?
pp
cresc.
A _ las, youth's radiant visions, O say, why must ye go?
cre - - scen - - do
f
Poco più animato.
Thus are my dreams of hap _ pi_ness ful_filled!
Poco più animato.
p

L.
To-day my troth un-to the Prince was plight-ed, the hus-band of my
poco cresc.
choice, One whose clev-er-ness, good looks, and noble birth, and riches,
cresc.
might well at-tract a wo-man of greater worth than I. Dis-tinguish'd,
mf
ff
f
chiv-al-rous, who can com-pare with him? Ah, none!
Then where-fore should I feel this sense of fear and gloom?
p
cre

riten.
Tempo I.
L.
I weep and trem - ble! O, burning tears of girl - hood, why
riten.
Tempo I.
-scen - do
f
pp
must ye flow? A - las, youth's radiant visions, ah, say, why
pp
pp
must ye go? A - las, youth's radiant visions, ah, say, why
cre - - scen - do
must ye go? Ah, say, why
f
p
(she weeps.)
must ye go?
espress.
pp

L.
I feel so
sad and fear_ful!
I strive in vain to cheat my heart!
I am a_
lone,
the world
is now a_sleep...
sfp
p
f
un poco accelerando
Poco più. (♩ = 76)
LISA (with passion).
O
Poco più.
p
f
p

L.
hear me, Night! To thee I may un-
fold the se-cret sor--row that chills my
youth. 'T is dark and sad as
Arpa.
Ob.
p
f
thou, 't is mourn---ful as his
Arpa.
p
poco cresc.
12

L.
ff
long - ing glan - - ces from eyes that
Arpa.
12
mf
rob me of my peace and glad - ness... O
Arpa.
7
Queen of Night! As dark, as
Arpa.
12
etc.
p
proud as thou! A fal - len an gel, to

me he seems, his eyes with
L.
wild and ard - ent pas - - - sion
L.
burn - - - ing!
Un poco stringendo.
p cre
A wond - rous dream
Un poco stringendo.
po
mf
pp
L.
scen do
pos - ess - es me, and all my soul is
co a
po
L.
thrall and cap - tive to its spell! O
co cre
scen

L.
ff
Night! O night!
Moderato. (♩ = 108)
(Herman appears at the door of the balcony. Lisa, dumb with terror, starts back. They stand silently gazing at each other. Lisa makes a movement as though to escape.)
Moderato.
ff
dim. poco a poco
riten molto
p
Andantino. (♩ = 84)
ad libitum
What brings you here, O rash and foolish man? Why
HERMAN.
Wait, but one moment, I must speak with you!
Andantino.
colla parte
f
p
mf

HERMAN.
(Lisa tries to go away.)
L.
seek me here? To say farewell!
Meno mosso. (♩= 66)
riten.
Adagio. (♩= 56)
H.
O, do not leave me thus! One mo_ment! Then I myself will go my way and leave you evermore in
peace... O spare one moment! 'tis so litt_le! A dy_ing man you see be_fore you.
Moderato con moto. (♩= 100)
LISA.
Now say, what brings you here? Then leave me!
No!
I'll call for help!
Call then.

(draws out a pistol.)
ad libitum
H.
and rouse the household I care not how I die, in pub_lic, or a_lone!
cresc.
colla parte
in tempo
(Lisa remains silent with bended head.)
in tempo
f
mf
dim.
Andante.
HERMAN.
But if your heart still holds a spark of hum an feel_ing, or of
Andante.
p

Moderato agitato. (♩ = 104)
H.
pit - - - y,
(passionately.)
you will not go,
Moderato agitato.
p molto espres.
pp
but hear my words! Good
LISA.
an - - - gels,
cre - - scen - do poco
L.
help me!
HERMAN
I come to you in this my life's last
a poco
H.
hour! To-day I learn'd that you had made your
mf
choice and plight - ed troth, al - as, for aye!
di - mi

Sostenuto
(with force and passion.)
H.
My doom un-kind - - ly seal - ing! Since I must
Sostenuto
nu - en - do
pp
die, be-stow on me one bless - ing, re-fuse me
po - co
not! Could I sur-vive the day that sees us
a po co cre -
part - ed for ev - er - more!
scen - do
mf
mf
ff
Yours was my life, and yours my

H.
wor - - ship, you were the
H.
one and on - ly dream that
mf
H.
filled my heart! The end has
H.
come, yet e'er I bid this
di - - mi - -

H.
world fare_well for ev - er, be_stow one
nu en
do
p
H.
pas - sing hour up_on my sor - row, Ah, let me
p
cre
H.
stay near you while night is still, and with your
scen
do
H.
beau - - - ty lull my an - - guish!
mf

H.
Then death may come and bring me peace!
(Lisa stands gazing sadly at Herman.)
Stay there! How
beau_ti_ful you are!
LISA. (with faltering voice.)
O leave me! O leave me!
HERMAN.
Thou art my queen! my goddess, my an - gel!
riten.
sf

Andante. (♩= 66)
(Herman kneels before her.)
HERMAN.
Forgive me, bright celestial vision, that I have spoilt
Andante.
H.
thy peace of mind, forgive, yet do not turn
animando
a-way in fear and
animando
an-ger, but to my grief be kind!
riten.
riten.
Tempo I.
O pit-y me,
Tempo I.
my life is ov-er, my dy-ing pray'r to thee I make, Look down, my love, look
down in pit-y, I per-ish for thy sake! Ah, if my soul is rack'd with anguish
string.
colla parte

Tempo I.
H.
'tis all for love of thee. My heart is we-ary, show com-passion. O
Tempo I.
mf
dim.
p
(Lisa weeps.)
shed one tear for me! Thou weepest! Thou?
piangendo
sfp
p
How may I read this sadness? For-give - ness? Yes, and
mf
dim
(He takes her hand which she does not withdraw.)
pit - y? God's angels bless thee, sweet!
stringendo
p
cre - scen - do
sempre-stringendo
cre - scen - do

Andante mosso. (♩ = 76)
HERM.
ff
Thou art my queen, my god - dess, my an -
Andante mosso.
ff
m.d.
m.g.
gel!
(embraces her)
stringendo
Allegro vivo. (♩ = 152)
(Sound of steps and a knock at the door.)
Allegro vivo.
p
sf
THE COUNT. (at the door).
Li - sa, op-en quick!
LISA (in agitation).
The Count - ess! Heav'n help us! I am un
done! The window! too late now! in here!
(The knocking grows louder. Lisa hides Herman behind a curtain.)
(Lisa goes to the door and
sffp

opens it. Enter the Countess in night attire, surrounded by maids with candles.)
COUNTESS.
What, not a_sleep? Not yet un_dress'd? What means this noise?
LISA (dumbfounded).
O grand-mamma, I could not get to sleep to night, I feel so rest_less...
Poco meno. (♩= 138)
COUNTESS (signs to her to shut the balcony door).
This door wide op_en still? Come, what's the mat_ter, child, what silly fancies!
Poco meno.
C.
what non_sense! 't is enough, now quick, to bed!

(taps with her walking stick.)
LISA.
C.
You hear me?
Yes, grand-mamma, I'll
p marcato
p
p
COUNTESS.
L.
go!
Not sleep - y!...
That's a pret - ty
C
stor - y!
Fine hours to keep!
Not sleep - y!
sfp
sfp 3
sfp 3
sfp 3
sfp 3
COUNT. (leav-
ing the room).
ad libitum
LISA.
ad libitum
ritenuto
C
To bed at once!
For-give me, I am go - ing!
I
ritenuto
sfp
sf
sfp
sfp
p
Allegro moderato. (♩= 120)
C.
heard a sud-den noise;
It start-led me from slumber!
Good night, child!
pp
pp

(Exit.)
C
Let's hear no more of all these sil_ly tricks!
mf
HERMAN.
When a third man impell'd by des_pair from thy bo_som the sec_ret shall
pp marcato
cre - - scen - - do
H.
tear of three cards, three cards, three-
H.
cards! I feel a deathlike chill that
pp pp
H.
runs through all my veins! O hid_eous spec_tre, Death, be gone, come not again!
riten.
ff
ff in tempo

(Lisa locks the door after the Countess and, approaching the balcony, opens it and makes a sign to order him out. Herman emmerges.)

ff
ff
HERMAN.
riten.
Moderato assai. (♩ = 84)
O Li-sa, pit-y me!
Just now it seem'd to me that
Moderato assai.
lar - ga - mente
p
cre
p
H.
death was my best friend, my one and last sal-va-tion, a wel-come re-fuge!
scen - do
mf
p
H.
Now all is changed! I fear his com-ing, I dread his pres - ence!
cre
scen - do
mf
p

H.
Now, you have giv'n me hope and cour - age, Now, I would
cresc.
cre
live and die for you a_lone!
LISA.
O poor, un_hap_py man!
scen - do
L.
Tell me, what can I do for you, how can I help you now?
HERMAN.
De- cide my fate at once!
LISA.
Ah, would you ru_in all my years! Nay,
leave me, I im - plore you, I com - mand you!
scen - do

Allegro giusto. (♩ = 120)
HERMAN.
A - las! To hear from you my cru-el doom and sen - tence! O heaven!
LISA.
Allegro giusto.
f
p
cre
scen
do
L.
Am I yield - ing?... If you love me, go!
HERMAN.
First
f
p
p
p
H.
speak that word: „die!"
LISA.
God, have mer - cy!
HERM.
Fare-
cre
scen
do
po
co
a
H.
well!
(Herman makes a movement to depart.)
stringendo
po
co
f
cre
scen

HERM. (seizes her in his arms and kisses her; she lets her head sink on his shoulder).
LISA.
a tempo
No, re - main! Be - lov - ed mine, my
a tempo
-do
ff
pp
LISA.
fff
I am
fff
queen, my an - - - - gel!
My love, my
f
Andante.
L.
yours!
H.
own!
(Curtain.)
Andante.
fff
m.d.
m.g.
fff
fff

End of Act I.

ACT II.

SCENE III.

№ 11. Entr'acte and Chorus.

p
pp
mp
mf
f

(Curtain.)

(A large reception room. A masked ball at the house of a rich dignitary. Theatrical boxes down the sides of the room between the columns. A quadrille in which young people in various costumes take part. *Contredanses.* A choir of singers, on a platform.)

CHOIR OF SINGERS.
Sopr.
Hap - py and bent on en - joy_ment,
Alti.
Ten.
Bas.
Hap - py, and bent on en _ joy _ ment, Friends,we have met here this eve_ning!

Friends, we have met here this eve_ning!
Hap - py and bent on en - joy - ment, friends, we have met here this eve_ning!
Put a_side troub_le and sad_ness, and join in the danc_es and
games!
games! and join in the danc_es and games! Drive a_
Drive a -
Drive a
Now join the games and
cresc.

way, drive a - way, all your care, and be
way, drive a - way, all your care, and be
way, drive a - way, all your care, and be
danc-es, join the danc - es, Drive a-way all care, Come, drive a - way all
gay! Drive a - way, drive a - way all your
gay! Drive a - way, drive a - way quick - ly
gay! Drive a - way, drive a - way all your
care, now join the games and join the danc-es, drive a - way all your care,

care and be gay! With fro - lic, and danc - ing, be hap - py,
all your care and be gay! With fro - lic, and danc - ing, be hap - py,
care and be gay! With fro - lic, and danc - ing, be
your care, and be gay! With fro - lic, and danc - ing, be
friends, to - day!
friends, to - day!
hap - py, friends, to - day!
hap - py, friends, to - day!

mf
Clap till your fing - ers are
mf
p
p
ting - ling,
mf
Go where the mask - ers are
mf
mf
Clap till your fing - ers are
ting - ling,
f
mf
f
p
ming - ling,
f
Fol - low the glance that gleams
f
mf
Go where the mask - ers are
ming - ling!
f
mf
f
mf

bright - est,
Mix where the laugh - ter rings
Fol - low the glance that gleams bright - est
light - est!
Choose out the maids that look
Mix where the laugh - ter rings light - est!
sweet - est,
Join in the dance that is
Choose out the maids that look sweet - est,

fleet - est,
Foot it in man - y a
Join in the dance that is fleet - est
measure, Drive a - way care, Wel - come pleas - ure!
Foot it in man - y a measure now wel - come to pleas - ure!
Foot it in man - y a measure, Drive a - way care, Wel - come
Foot it in man - y a meas - ure, Now wel - come to

pleas - ure! Our host and his wife bid each guest, Take
part in the sport he likes best, Be
wel - come! Our host bids each guest Take

part in the sport he likes best, Most wel - come, Most
wel - come each guest, Most wel - come, most wel - come each
guest!
(Enter the Master of the Ceremonies.)

№ 12. Scene and Aria: The Prince.

Lo stesso tempo.
THE MASTER OF THE CEREMONIES.
Our nob_le host in_vites you all to come this way;
Lo stesso tempo.
PIANO.
M.C.
He has pre_pared a pi_ro_tech_ni_cal dis_play.
Moderato. (♩=100.)
Moderato.
TCHEKALINSKY.
Our Herman does not seem quite hap_py; I'll wag_er he has fall'n in
(All the guests flock to the terrace in the garden.)
T.
love, Some_times he's nice, and sometimes snap_py.
SOURIN.
No,

S.
'tis not love that makes him glum. What think you fills his
cresc.
mf
p
p
S.
mind? Guess? The se - cret of those three
TCHEK.
TOMSKY.
S
cards! What! The fool! I scarce - ly can be - lieve this stor - y, he
cresc.
mf
p
SOURIN.
TOMSKY.
T.
is no fool! Can it be true? He told me so him - self. In jest!

TCHEK. (to Sourin.)
(Exeunt.)
We'll see! Lets play on him some trick!
TOMSKY.
Yet tru - ly, he's so made, that what he longs for, must be
cresc.
mf
p
T.
(Exit.)
his at once! Poor fel - lew, poor Her - man!
(The room is empty. Enter attendants who prepare the stage for the Interlude.)

Quasi andante. (♩ = 88)
THE PRINCE.
Quasi andante.
(Enter the Prince and Lisa.)
You are so si_lent, dearest
espress.
mf
p
mf
Poco più animato.
LISA.
P.
Lis_a, what trou_ble weighs up_on your heart? Con_fide in me! Not
Poco più animato.
p
p
p
(Strives to go.)
THE PRINCE.
L.
now, dear Prince, to_morrow... Ex_cuse me! One mo_ment,
cre- scen- do
Andante. (♩ = 72)
riten.
P.
Stay a lit_tle lon_ger! Ah, Lis_a, let me tell you
Andante.
riten.
f
mf
p
p
a tempo
con grandezza
P.
all! I love you,
a tempo

Andantino mosso. (♩ = 80)
P.
dear, be_yond all reck'ning, I think of you by day and night, For
Andantino mosso.
p
you my life I'd lay down glad_ly, For you a_gainst the world I'd
mp
fight, Yet hear me, child, your heart shall keep its free_dom, Your
p
life to mine I ne'er will chain, I could re_nounce you, for your
f
poco cresc.
mf
own sake, and tram_ _ _ple down my jea_lous pain. For
decresc.

Un poco più animato.
P.
you, for you, all things were eas - - y. Not on - - ly as my wife I'd
Un poco più animato.
love you, Of your least wish I'd be the
slave,— I long to be your friend and
guard - - ian, Tend - - - er to
cher-ish and to save! I think my
riten.
riten.

Tempo I.
eyes for love of you were blind_ed, but now at last, the
truth is clear, To you I seem a kind_ly stran_ger, You
would not have me draw too near! O, let me break these cru_el
affettuoso
bar_riers, I feel for you with all my heart, But
cresc.
Poco più mosso.
yet no com _ fort can I give you, while thus you grieve and weep a_
riten.
più f
mf
ff

a tempo
riten.
P.
part. O, let me break these cru_el barriers, I feel for you with all my
a tempo
p
riten.
a tempo
P.
heart. I love you, dear, be_yond all reck' ning, I
a tempo
p
dolce
P.
think of you by day and night. For you my life I'd lay down
P.
glad _ ly, For you a_gainst the world I'd fight! O
(Exeunt.)
P.
dear _ est heart, con _ fide in me!
riten.
p

№13. Scene.

(Enter Herman in costume, but without a mask, carrying in his hand a letter.)
Moderato assai. (♩ = 88)
HERMAN.
Moderato assai.
PIANO.
p
p
HERMAN (reads). After the performance wait for me in the room. I must speak with you...
H.
sfp
p
H.
The sight of her will give me courage to cast aside this thought.
(sits down.)
sfp
dolce
p
H.
a piacere
Three
cre - - scen - - do
sf
sfp
H.
cards!
Could I but know them, what wealth were mine!
f
p

ad libitum
H.
and then with her I might take flight, far from the world...
colla parte
(A few guests return to the room; among them Tchekalinsky and
Damn_a - tion! but the thought drives me to mad - ness!
Sourin. They perceive Herman, approach him stealthily, and finally whisper behind him.)
TCHEKALINSKY.
Are you then that third man,
SOURIN.
Are you then that third man, im_pell'd by des_
marcato
po - co a po - co

cresc.
riten.
T.
im_pell'd by des_pair, Who longs in her se_cret to share? „Three cards, three cards, three
S.
cresc.
pair, Who longs in her se_cret to share? „Three cards, three cards, three
riten.
cresc.
mf riten.
T.
cards?"... (They conceal themselves.)
S.
cards?"... a tempo
(Herman gets up from his seat with a bewildered air,
sf
p
p
cresc.
as though he did not understand what had happened. He looks around, but Tchek. and Sourin are now lost in the crowd.)
f
TCHEK.
ff „Three cards, three cards, three cards!" (Laughter.)
SOURIN.
ff „Three cards, three cards, three cards!"
A FEW VOICES FROM THE CHORUS. Ten.
(Laughter.)
Bass.
ff
„Three cards, three cards, three cards!"
f
mf

(They mingle with the guests who are gradually returning to the room.)
dolce
HERMAN.
What was it? A joke? Or some il lusion? No!
H.
Meno mosso, adagio. (♩ = 60)
If it were true? (Buries his head in his hands.)
O,
Meno mosso, adagio.
sf
sfp
(remains lost in thought.)
MASTER OF THE CEREMONIES.
fol _ ly, my reas _ on tot.ters!
f Our.
ad libitum
host now prays you all to take your seats, to see a pret_ty past_or_ al called „The faith.ful
p colla parte

№ 14. Interlude „The faithful Shepherdess."

a) Chorus of Shepherds and Shepherdesses.

Allegro vivace. (♩ = 100)
THE MASTER OF THE CEREMONIES.
Shepherdess.
(The guests occupy the places prepared for them.)
Allegro vivace.
PIANO.
p
p
cre - scen - do po - co a po - co
f
(Youths and maidens dressed as shepherds and shepherdesses appear on the scene which represents a
f
meadow Dances and games.)

CHORUS OF SHEPHERDS AND SHEPHERDESSES.
Be
side this peace_ful stream_let, Be_neath these shad_y trees, We shep_herds oft as_
(During the singing of this chorus a Round is danced. Chloë alone does not join in the dance, but sits apart, looking glum, and twining a garland.)

sem - ble and giad - ly take our ease. Some - times we nimb - ly
foot it, And sing a round - e - lay, Or rest - ing, twinebright
gar lands From blos - som of the may!
We dance and gai - ly
mf

and sing a round - e - lay,
foot it,
Or rest - - ing, twine bright
tr
f
from blossoms of the the may!
gar - lands
Be - side this peace - ful
tr
f
Cor.
f
Be - neath these shad - y trees,
We shep-herds oft as -
stream-let,
f

sem - ble, And glad - - ly take our ease, We
shep_herds oft as_ sem - ble and glad - - ly take our ease!
f
f

b) Dance of Shepherds and Shepherdesses.

(Shepherds and Shepherdesses retire to the back of the stage.)

c) Duet of Chloë and Daphnis.

Larghetto. (♪= 108)
CHLOË.
Larghetto. (Marquez 4 temps dans chaque mesure.)
dolce
PIANO.
p
mf
Ch.
p
pp
A
las! My chos - en swain, For whom I sigh in vain, Who
sempre staccato l'accompagnamento
has my heart in keep - ing, For whom these tears I'm weep - ing, Ah,
p

Ch.
comes no more to dance, Ah, comes no
sfp
pp
p
sfp
DAPHNIS.
(Pauline) (Enter Daphnis)
Ch.
more to dance! 'Tis I, but filled with an-guish, O'er-
pp
p
D.
come by bashful-ness! No long-er will I languish, My
p
p
D.
pas-sion I'll con-fess, No long-er will I lan-guish,
mf
D.
My passion I'll con-fess. No more I'll lan-guish,
mf
p
mf

CHLOË.
Ah, leave me not a
D.
my passion I'll con - fess! I've loved you many a day,
p
p
pp
Ch.
gain, My dear-est Shep - herd - swain, With -
D.
day, With - out you life was grey, You
Ch.
out you I was wear - y, With - out you life is
D.
knew not how I yearn'd, love, Your smiles from me you
p
Ch.
drear - y, Ah, why I can - - not say! Ah,
D.
turn'd, love! Why did you look a - way? Why
sfp
pp

Ch.
why I can - - not say!
I know not, I know not why 't is
D.
did you look a - way?
I know not,
I know not why 't was
sfp
pp
pp
Ch.
so,
I know not,
I know not why 't is
so!
riten.
D.
so,
I know not,
I know not why 't was
so!
riten.
mf
mf
f
ff

d) Finale.

Tempo di minuetto. (♩ = 72)
p
tr
più f
(Enter the attendants of Plutus, bearing costly gifts. Dance.)
mf
tr
p
tr
più f
mf
f
tr
Fl.
p
p
p
mf
f
(Enter Plutus.)

PLUTUS (Tomsky).
Fair Shep_herd_ess, I pray you, Which hus_band shall it
tr
p
più f
P.
be? This shep _ herd youth or me, who wins your
mf
tr
DAPHNIS.
P.
love? How say you? My heart and I a -
tr
p
D.
gree, There's but one love for me, This
tr
più f
D.
maid for whom I yearn, for whom my heart doth
mf
tr

Lo stesso tempo. (♩=♩)
D.
burn.
I have but one po
PLUTUS.
My cof - fers are not emp - ty, I've
Lo stesso tempo. (♩=♩)
p
D.
ses - sion: True love is all I've got, is all I've
P.
prec - ious stones in plent - y, And piles of gleam - ing
D.
got,
Sweet Chlo - - ë make con -
P.
gold! No gem, but you shall wear it, I'll

D.
fes - sion: Wilt share my hum - ble cot, my hum - ble cot? Fresh
P.
give you wealth un - told. My king - dom, you shall share it, One
D.
flow'rs and rib - ands bright Our sim - ple tastes de light, We
P.
half shall be your own, I of - fer you a throne!
D.
need no cost - ly treasures, Nor seek lux - ur - ious pleasures, My
P.
My cof - fers are not emp - ty, I've prec - ious stones in
cresc.

D.
gift shall be a crown of blossoms fresh_ly blown. We
P.
plen_ty and piles, and piles, of gleaming gold!
mf
p
pp
D.
need no cost_ly treasures, Nor seek lux_ur_ious pleasures, My
P.
No gem, but you shall wear it, I'll give you wealth un_
pp
cresc.
D.
gift shall be a crown of blossoms fresh_ly blown!
P.
told, I'll give you, I'll give you wealth un_told!
mf
p
pp

CHLOË.
I ask no wed - ding pre - sent Of
Ob.
p
Ch.
jew - els rich and rare, My shep - herd's hut is
Ch.
bare, But love can make it pleas - ant, but
ff
cresc.
Ch.
love can make it pleas - ant! And
mf
f

(Turns to Daphnis.)
Ch.
so, Sir, fare you well! With you I fain would dwell!
f
Ch.
Go now, and gather pos_ies and with a crown of
p
f
p
Ch.
ro_ses, My con_stan_cy re_pay, My con_stan_cy re_
f
p
f
p
ad libit.
Ch.
pay, We'll plight our troth to

 39106

Larghetto. (Come prima.) CHLOE.
day!
DAPHNIS Be - hold a hap - py lov - er, My
Larghetto. (Come prima.) Be - hold a hap - py lov - er, My
Ch.
doubts and fears are ov - er, Now swift - ly let time
D
doubts and fears are ov - er, Now swift - ly let time
Ch.
run, Till you and I are one, till you
D.
run, Till you and I are one, till you
Ch.
and I are one, till you and I are
D.
and I are one, till you and I are

Un pochettino più vivo. (♩ = 116)
Ch.
one, are one!
D.
one, are one!
CHORUS OF SHEPHERDS AND SHEPHERDESSES.
Un pochettino più vivo.
His doubts and fears are ov - - er And swift the hours will
Un pochettino più vivo.
run, Un - til this hap - py lov - er And his true maid are

one, and his true maid are
one, and his true maid are
Più vivo. (♩ = 100)
one!
(Enter Amor and Hymen who crown the happy pair.)
Più vivo.
p
sf
p
p

3
sf
p

Poco più. (♩ = 112)
Allegro vivo.
Tempo del Imo Coro.

(Chloë and Daphnis dance hand in hand. The Shepherds and Shepherdesses follow their example and dance a Round.)

ff
The sun on them is shin - ing, And Zeph - yr soft - ly
blows. Once more a - mong the shep - herds, Our Daph - nis glad - ly
goes! His doubts and fears are ov - er, His woo - ing bold - ly

done, O, hap - py shep-herd lov - er Who such a bride has
won!
And Zeph yr soft - ly
won! The sun on them is shin - ing
blows!
Our Daph - nis glad - ly
Once more a - mong the shep - herds,
mf
f
tr

goes!
His woo_ing bold_ly
His doubts and fears are ov_er
f
Cor.
f
done,
O, hap_py shep_herd lov_er, Who such a bride has
ff
won!
O hap_py shep_herd lov_er, who such
f

a bride has won! who such a bride has won, who
such a bride has won! (They walk off the stage in couples.)
ff

End of Interlude

№ 15. Closing scene.

Allegro moderato. (♩ = 120)
PIANO.
(At the end of the Interlude some of the guests rise, some remain in their seats, talking with
animation. Herman comes to the front of the stage.)
HERMAN (lost in thought).
„A third man im-pell'd by his love!"
H.
(He turns and sees the Countess
Well? Am I not in love? Yes, madly! Ha!
before him. Both shudder, and remain gazing at each other.)
poco a poco cre - scen - do

SOURIN (masked).
Be_hold, there stands your destin'd
p
(He laughs and glides away).
S.
love!
HERMAN.
A_gain... the voice....
pp
pp
H.
Fear grips me! Theselfsamevoice, Whoseis it? Devil's, or
po - co a po - co cre - - scen -
H.
man's? And why shouldhe thus fol - - low me a
- do
H.
ad libit.
bout? Damn_a_tion! O, how I suf_fer, wretched fool!
ff
ff
mf

Andante. (♩= 72)
(Enter Lisa, masked.)
LISA.
Now list - en, Herman!
Andante.
pp
HERMAN.
You, you. at last!
How glad I am that you are
p
H.
here! I love you!
I love you!
LISA.
Not
più f
L.
now! Not here! 'T was not for this I came to seek you!... Take this!
dim.
pp
L.
It is the garden key... You know the entrance.. A ladder's there...
pp

L.
HERMAN.
by that you'll reach to grand - mam - ma's own room... What! Her own
H.
LISA.
room? She'll not be there herself... but near her por - trait you'll
più f
pp
L.
find a door... it leads to me! For I am
L.
yours and yours a - lone, be - lov - ed... yours a - lone!
f
pp
pp
L.
Our fate we must de - cide... to - mor - row... my dear - est,

HERMAN.
L.
my lov - er! No! Not to - mor - row! No!
LISA (alarmed).
HERMAN.
to - night I will be there... But, Her - man - Come I
f
p
LISA.
H.
must! Well, if you wish it! I am your humb - le
(Hides herself.)
HERMAN.
L.
slave! Goodbye... It is not I, but fate it - self that wills it, I
mf
p
cre - scen - do
(Goes away in haste.)
H.
am to learn the se - cret!
f
ff

Allegro. (♩= 132)
MASTER. (Enter the Master of the Ceremonies, excited and breathless.)
Her gracious Ma_jest _ y has just an_nounced that she is coming...
Allegro.
pp
pp
(Much excitement among the chorus. M. of C. divides the crowd so that a way is made for the Empress down the centre)
CHORUS OF GUESTS.
The Empress! the Empress!
The Empress! the Empress!
Her gracious Ma_jest _ y will grace the party... Our host indeed is
The Empress, the Empress! Will grace the party... Our host indeed is
Our host indeed is for _ tu_nate to have this honour, And
Our host in _ deed is for_tu _ nate to have this hon _ our, And
for _ tu_nate to have this hon_our! What a joy for us our Empress here to
for _ tu_nate!... to have this hon _ our! Ah, what a joy for
mf

what a hap_pi_ness for us! This crowns a brilliant en_ter_
greet! No, he's in
us! She brings the French am_bas_sa_dor! This
p
MASTER OF CEREMONIES (to singers).
The
tain_ment! What great de_light, what loy_al feeling!
Par_is! Prince Fred' rick! He adds still greater lus_tre!
adds more brilliance than be_fore! A rout so splendid we rare_ly
cre - - scen -

c.
Song of greeting be pre - par - ing!
cresc.
This re - cep - tion is per - fect!
cresc.
This re - cep - tion's per - fect, is per - fect!
cresc.
Now sing „Hail to thee!" This is
cresc.
wit - ness! Now sing „Hail to thee!"
- do po - - co a po - - co
Now sing „Hail to thee!" She comes, she comes, she comes!
per - fect! She comes, she comes, she comes!
This re - cep - tion's perfect! See, there she comes, she comes! See our

ff
ff Emp ress and mo - ther, Glor - ious Tsar - it - - sa!
ff
ff
f cre - - scen - - do
(All turn towards centre door.)
ff
(Master of Ceremonies makes sign to the singers to begin.)
riten. molto

CHORUS OF GUESTS AND SINGERS.
Andante assai maestoso. (♩ = 72)
Hail to thee, Ye_ka_te_ri_na!
Mo_ther of our Rus_sian
Andante assai maestoso.
land!
Hail to thee, Ye_ka_te_ri_na!
Mo_ther of our Rus_sian land!
Mo_ther of our Rus_sian

(The gentlemen make their lowest court bow.)
fff
land!
Mo_ther of our Rus_sian land! All hail!
(The ladies make a profound curtsey.)
(Enter pages, two and two.)
All hail!
All hail! All hail!
(Curtain.)

End of Third Scene.

SCENE IV.

The Countess's bedroom, lit with lamps.

№ 16. Scene and Chorus.

mf
p
(Curtain.)
pp
più f
cresc.
f

p
pp
pp
pp
pp
(Enter Herman through the secret door. He looks round the room.)
p
pp
pp

HERMAN.
Ah
H.
yes, 't is all as Lis _ a told me...
H.
Well then? Does cour _ age fail me? Nay!
H.
Now is my chance! I soon shall wring the secret from the

H.
Countess!
(He appears lost in thought.)
pp
HERMAN.
Suppose there is no se_cret? And all should prove to be the
p
H.
fan_cy of my fev'rish brain?
(He goes to the door of Lisa's room. Then he stands before the portrait of the Countess.)
p
(Midnight strikes.)
p
più f
f
mf
f
mf

dim.
Poco meno. (♩= 66)
HERMAN.
Yes, there she is, „the Ve - nus of
Poco meno.
p
più f
H.
Mos-cow!" What dark mys - ter - ious pow - er has linked our fates to -
p espress.
H.
geth - er? Bringst thou my end, or do I bring thee thine? I know too well
più f
cresc.

H.
that one of us deals death and ru - in to the oth - er!
f
f
più f
di - mi - nu - en - do
HERMAN.
I gaze up - on thy face and I should hate it...
p
H.
but yet I can - not turn a - way mine eyes!
mp
p
H.
ad libit.
'Twere well if I could flee, but power
mf cresc.
ff

Moderato. (♩ = 100)
H
fails me... Her pierc - ing glance, where'er I turn it,
Moderato.
p
fol - lows and trou - bles me... A strange, un - can - ny
f
Tempo I. (♩ = 76)
being! Well! It was fate or -
Tempo I.
p
dain'd our meet - ing... 't was de - creed!
più f
mf
di - mi - nu - èn - do

pp
HERMAN. Allegro moderato (♩ = 116)
H.
Hark!
now some one comes!...
Allegro moderato.
pp
pp
Steps!
Yes! Well, so
(He hides behind the curtains of the boudoir.)
be it!
p
p
(A maid comes in hastily and lights the candles. She is followed by other maids and dependants.)
mp
mp
mf
(Enter the Countess who is at once surrounded and fussed over by the maids and dependants.)
mf

Sop.
CHORUS OF MAIDS AND DEPENDANTS.
Alt.
mf
Yes, our
mf
gra - cious ben - efact - ress al - ways is in such re-quest, Ah, we
p
fear she is tir'd, read - y now to seek her rest!
Is she
più f
Is she quite worn out? Yes, we're cer - tain
quite worn out? But we're cer - tain, that few
p

that few la - dies at the ball, Al-though p'rhaps
la - dies at the ball, Though p'rhaps young - er than our Count - ess could com -
young - er than our Count - ess, could com - pare with her at all! Yes, our
(off the stage)
pare with her at all, her at all! Yes, our
(They escort the Countess to the boudoir.)
cresc.
mf
p
staccato
gra - cious ben - e - fact - ress al - ways is in such re - quest, Ah, we
p
(Enter Lisa and her maid, Mary.)
fear that she's tir'd, read - y now to seek her rest!
pp

LISA.
No, Mar - y, you need not come!
MARY.
What can be wrong with you, you look pale, Miss!
cre - - scen - do
LISA.
No, I am well...
MARY (guessing the truth).
Ah, Heav'ns a - bove!
mf
p
M.
can that be it?
LISA.
Yes! He will
cre - - scen -
come... be sil - ent, per - haps he now is there and a -
do

L.
waits me... Do not be_tray us, Mar_y! Be my
espress.
mf
friend.
'Twas his de_
MARY.
Ah! should mis_for_tune come to you!
f
p
sire, and since I choose him to be my lord and mas_ter I
mf
must o_bey his least com_mand_ment He is my fate, my des_ti_
ad libit.
f

Tempo I.
(Exeunt.)
L.
ny!
CHOR.
Sop
(The maids and dependants bring the Countess back to her room. She is in night attire and wears a night cap. They prepare her bed.)
mf
Ben - e-
Tempo I.
pp
mf
pp
Sop.
fac - tress a-dored, you will soon feel re-stored, You are
Alt.
mf
Ben - e-fac - tress a - dored, you will soon feel re-
pp
wear - y no doubt, By en - gage-ments quite worn out! Ben - e-
stored, You are wear - y no doubt, and quite worn out!
pp
fac - tress a-dored, you will soon feel re-stored! Now re-
Ben - e-fac - tress a - dored, you will soon feel re-stored

tire and rest till morn, then wake re_freshed, Like
Rest till morn - ing, then a_wake re_freshed, like
pp poco cresc.
flow'rs by dawn made bright! Now re_
flow'rs by dawn made bright!
mf
tire and rest till morn, then wake re_freshed like
Rest till morn - ing, then a_wake re_freshed, like
pp poco cresc.
flow'rs by dawn made bright! Gra_ cious
flow'rs by dawn made bright!
mf
pp

ben - e-fac-tress, now re - tire to rest, now good-
Gra-cious ben - e-fac-tress, now re-tire to rest,
pp
night, now good-night, now good...
now good-night, now good-night, now good...
COUNTESS.
Stop this rub-bish, for it bores me! I am
sf
mf
p
C.
wear - - y, tired out!

(The Maids settle her on a couch and prop her up with cushions.)
C.
I will not go to bed just yet!
p
mf
p
p
cresc.
COUNTESS.
ad libit.
Ah! How stale the world has
f
Andantino con moto. (♩ = 84)
C.
grown! Yes, now-a-days I think so-ci-et-y has lost its
Andantino con moto.
pp
pp
C.
brilliance. Such shock-ing man- - - ners! Such bad style!
pp

C.
I nev - er meet a soul who dan - ces well, or
dim.
mp
sings with ex - pres - sion! Who can dance? Who can sing?
p
pp
riten.
Poco meno (♩ = 76)
The girls! And yet for - mer - ly, What dancers then! What
Poco meno.
pp
singers! Le duc d'Or - lé - ans; le duc d'Ayen,
ppp
duc de Coigny... La comtesse d'Estrades, la duchesse de Brancas...
sempre pp

C
Dear, dear, what fam - ous names! And some - times, sometimes she, herself,
her-self, Mar-quise de Pom-pa - dour!...
Andante sostenuto: (♩=66)
And I...
un poco marcato il tema
cre - scen - do
mf
pp
and I, sang be - fore them... le duc de la Val-lière once prais'd my voice!
Once, it was at Chan-til - ly, at Prince de Con-dé's, the
ppp
un poco marcato il tema
pp
King himself was there!
riten.
It seems but yest-er-day...

(OBSERVATION: The following song is borrowed from Grétry's opera „Richard Coeur de Lion.")
Andantino. (♩ = 76)
C.
Je crains de lui par - ler la nuit, j'é - cou - te
Andantino.
pp
pp
trop tout ce qu'il- dit... Il me dit: je vous ai - me, et je sens mal - gré
moi, je sens mon coeur qui bat, qui bat, je ne sais pas pour - quoi! Il
pp
1.
Più mosso. (As though waking from a dream and looking around her.)
(Maids and dependants
2.
quoi! Well, what are you all doing? Go, and leave me!
Più mosso.
f
mf
mf
mf
p
move away on tiptoe.)
(The Countess dozes off.)
Andantino. (♩ = 84)
pp
pp
pp
sf

COUNTESS.
Andante. (♩ = 69)
(Singing as though in her sleep.)
Je crains de lui par_ler la nuit, j'é_cou_te trop tout ce qu'il dit...
Andante.
riten.
meno.
Il me dit: je vous ai_me et
meno.
molto riten.
je sens mal_gré moi, je sens mon coeur qui bat, qui bat... je ne sais pas
molto riten.
Andante. (♩ = 72)
pour_quoi.....
Andante.

№ 17. Closing scene.

Moderato assai. (♩= 92)
PIANO.
pppp
mp
pp
mf
f
(Herman enters and stands looking at the Countess. She awakes, and struck with terror, her lips move without uttering a word.)
f
mf
p
cre
scen - do -
ff
HERMAN.
Countess,
Andante mosso. (♩= 76)
H.
do not fear! I implore you be not frightened!
Andante mosso.
p
p

H
See, I will not do youharm! I have
H.
come here to entreat one fav _ our you cangrant!
(The Countess continues to stare at Hermann and mumble as before.)
'Tis
pp
ad libitum
in tempo
yourstomakemerich and hap _ pyallmy life _ time! Mygood
colla parte
in tempo
ad libitum
in tempo
for_tune willbut cost you a few words! You
colla parte
in tempo

(The Countess raises herself a little.)
H.
know those names, three cards...
Ah, for whom would you guard the
secret?...
(Herman goes down on his knees.)
Poco meno. (♩= 69
If you have once known the ar - dour of pas - sion ate love,
Poco meno.
cresc.
If you re member the glow and the leap of young blood in spring,

H.
If you re-call how a child could soft-en your look by its plead - ing,
If you still keep a heart, a hu-man heart in your bos - om, Ah,
animando un poco.
now I ad-jure you, by all you cher - ish'd, as
Tempo I.
maid, as wife, as mo - ther, Aye, by all you hold as most sa - cred,
O tell me, reveal it, O tell me, tell me your se -
po - co - a
po - co cre scen - do

H.
riten.
cret! What use can it be, what use can it
p
più f
riten.
Poco più. (♩. = 84)
H.
p
be? Or per-chance, 't is
Poco più.
pp
pp
H.
linked to some old sin, to some deed of dark-ness,
H.
Then you stand in per-il of Hell and all its tor-ments?

H
Con_si_der well, your age now, and time is fly_ing fast,
H.
cresc.
Yet I will glad_ly take your sin on me!
mf
f
H.
f
Con_fess to me! re_veal it!
f
p
f
p
(The Countess pulls herself up on the couch and looks menacingly at Herman.)
H.
f
f

HERMAN.
H.
Speak, you old witch! Speak, or I will force you to
(He draws out a pistol.)
H.
tell me the truth!
(The Countess nods her head at him, and throws up her arms to protect herself from the shot, then
cresc.
falls back dead.)

Più andante. (♩= 72)
riten.
pp
(Herman bends over her corpse and seizes her by the hand.)
pp
pp
HERMAN.
H.
Come, have done with this pretence! Now name them to me quick_ly, three cards?..
pp
Yes or no?
O, she is
riten.
pp
ppp
Celli
C. B.
Moderato assai. (♩= 92)
dead! Too late! The se_cret with her
Moderato assai.
p
per_ished!
(Stands as though turned to stone.)
mf

HERMAN.
She's dead!
The se_cret with her
H.
per_ished...
she
is
dead!
She
is
H.
dead!
(Enter Lisa with a light.)

Vivace. (alla breve.) (𝅗𝅥 = ♩ = 92)
LISA.
(Catching sight of Herman.)
Why this noise? You! you, here?
Vivace. (alla breve.)
fp molto agitato
HERM. (Rushes towards her in fear and agitation).
Be still! Be still! for she is
dead, the se - cret now has per - - ished!
marcato
LISA.
HERM. (Points to the corpse).
Who is dead? O Heav'n, what words are these?
Too late!

(Lisa throws herself upon the body of the Countess.) LISA
H.
for she is dead, the se - cret with her per - - ished. Yes!
marcato
L.
She is dead! God help us! And
p
(Sobs.) HERMAN.
L.
this has been your work! Ah, no,
H.
I did not wish her death! I on - ly

LISA.
tried to learn the three cards! T'was that
which brought you here, not love of me! You
longed for those three cards! My love was nothing worth beside three cards... O, wretch-ed,
p
più f
più f
p
espress. poco a poco cresc.
marcato

L.
wretch - ed girl! A - las! Why did I
love you, who brought me shame and
marcato
mf
ru - in... O, heart - less man,
(Herman tries to speak, but she motions him with a stern gesture towards the secret door.)
be - tray - er! Murd' rer!

L.
Go! go! be gone! Go!
Go!
(Herman goes quickly away. Lisa sinks weeping beside the corpse of the Countess.)
HERMAN.
And she is dead!
marcato
(Curtain.)

END OF SECOND ACT.

ACT III.

SCENE V.

№ 18. Entr'acte and scene.

più f
pesante
m.g.
Ob.
cresc. in la mano diritta
marcatissimo
dim.

p
cresc.
sempre staccato
(Curtain.)
mf
dim.
(Herman's quarters in the barracks.)
p
(It is late evening and the moonlight gleams through the window from time to time. The wind howls outside.)
Drum.
(bugle call.)
pp
pp
(Herman seated at the table reading a letter
by the light of a candle.)
Cl.
pp
HERMAN (reads).
I do not believe you meant to kill the Countess....
I am wretched, believing I have wronged you....

Set me at rest! Today I will expect you on the Quay,
when no one will be there to see us. By midnight,
if you fail to come, I shall be filled with dreadful fears,
which I strive now to chase away. Forgive me, I suffer greatly...
HERMAN.
Poor woman!
Cl. basso
mf
H.
To what dark depths of shame and grief I've dragged her with me!
p
H.
p
(Falls back in his chair and is lost in revery.)
H.
Ah, could I find some quiet, some o - bliv - ion!
sfp
p
p

HERM. (Starts up in terror).
It haunts my wak-ing, at night it
Sopr.
Alt.
CHORUS OF SINGERS.
(Chorus off the stage. It must sing loud but from a distance.)
Gra - - - cious Lord, to
Ten.
Bass.
H.
comes in dreams, the dark, de-pres-sing pic-ture of her bur-ial, keeps
Thee I cry,

H.
rising up before me where'er I am...
My of - - fen - - - - ces, O
(Listens.)
H.
purge Thou a - way,

H.
What is that? Voi-ces, or the howling wind? I know not...
Lest the ev - - - il one pre-vail a - gainst my
sf p
H.
The same sad chant... yes, yes, they sing!
soul;
Lest I

H.
And there's the cha - pel, and the crowd, the cand - les and the
fall cap - - - tive to the
H.
cen - sers, sounds of weep - ing, the cat - a - falque, the
pow'rs of Hell, Lord for - -

H.
vault... and there she lies, the Count - ess, cold and breathless, still for
give, Lord - - - - - for - - - give the
H.
ev - er... Some un - known force com - pell'd my feet to
wick - - ed - ness of thy

 39106

fol - low in that black pro - cess - ion! Hor - ror! And
ser - - - vant, of thy
yet the will failed me to re - turn!...
ser - - vant!
Viole.
pp

H.
up - on her pal - lid face I gazed... and
pp
H.
then, she smil'd, a lit - tle wick - ed smile, and blink'd her
H.
eyes at me! Go, fear - ful ap - par
CHORUS
ff
ff
And
ff
ff
cre - scen - do
f

(Sinks back in his chair, hiding his face in his hands.)
H.
i - tion! Go!
grant her peace e - ter - - - - - -
nal!
fff

Moderato con moto. (♩= 112.)
PIANO.
pp
ppp
(A knock on the window. Herman raises his head and listens. The wind howls.)
pp ma un poco marcato
f
(Some one looks in at the window, then vanishes.)
dim.
pp
ppp
(The tapping at the window is heard again. A great gush
pp marcato
of wind blows it open and a shadow is seen there. The candle goes out.)
f

scen
cre
pp
do
fff
HERMAN. (Stiff with fright.)
Strange
H.
ter - rors seize me!
pp
cresc.
H.
mf

cresc.
HERMAN.
There... there... it comes!
mf
dim.
H.
See, now the door is opening... No!
mf
dim.
(He makes for the door, but the Countess's ghost bars his way.)
No! I can bear no more!
mf
dim.
f
ff

Andante non tanto. (♩= 84.)
fff
(He draws back, but the ghost approaches.)
fff
sf
sf
sf
sf
GHOST OF THE COUNTESS.
Against my will
pp
marcato
pp
sempre pp ma marcato in la mano sinistra
G.C.
I ap - pear,
I am sent that you may

G.C.
gain your dea-rest wish.
Now rescue Lis - - a,
and mar - ry her,
then three cards,
three cards,
three cards
shall bring you good for - tune.
Re -
mem - ber!
Three!
un po - co cresc.
ppp
marcato
ppp

G.C.
Sev
- en!
Ace!
ppp
Three!
semp - re ppp
(Vanishes.)
Sev - en!
Ace!
HERMAN. (With wild looks.)
Three!
semp - re ppp

H.
Sev - en!
Ace!
H.
Three!
Sev - en!
H.
Ace!
(Curtain.)
pppp

End of Fifth Scene.

SCENE VI.

№20. Scene and Arioso: Lisa.

Night. The canal opposite the Winter Palace. In the back ground the Quays of the Neva, and the Peter-and-Paul Fortress in the moonlight. Under the arch, in a dark corner, sits Lisa, dressed in black

LISA.

'T will soon be mid - night now, and

L.

Her - man not here, not here.

cresc.

L.
Ah, sure-ly he will
come to set at rest my an-guish.
p
f marcato
mf
'Twas fate that lured him on.
sf
A crime so hate-ful he could not, he could not, per-pe

L.
trate!
p
mf
O, I am wea - ry and out - worn with grief.
Andante molto cantabile. (♩ = 66)
Andante molto cantabile.
Ah, I am worn with my sor - row...
mf
p
pp
Ev - er in sight, morning and night, Crushing my heart like a heav - y stone...
Past days of glad - ness, O whith - er flown? Ah, I am wear - y, and

L.
all a - lone!
Once life was radiant with
mf
pp
p
prom - ise,
Then came black care,
Woe and des - pair,
Shat-t'ring the hopes that I cher - ish'd.
For-tune and love, both have
per - ish'd!
ff
Ah, I am worn by my sor - - row!
Ev - er in sight, morn - ing and night,
Ah,
cre - scen - do
dim.

Poco string.
riten.
L.
Crush-ing my heart like a heav - y stone. Past days of glad-ness, O
Poco string.
riten.
pp cresc.
mf dim.
whi - ther flown? Now comes black care, neg - lect and des - pair,
Tempo I.
Tempo I.
pp
mf
Shat - t'ring the hopes that I cher - - ish'd!
cantabile
p
O, I am wear - y! My life is
drear - y, And all my love and joy have per - ish'd...
riten.
pp
ppp

 39106

№ 21. Scene and Duet.

Moderato mosso. (♩ = 104)
LISA.
What if the clock strike midnight, thus ans'wring me that he is guilt - y
Moderato mosso.
PIANO.
p
and a murd' - rer? I dare not think of it!
cresc.
f
O, time,
(The clock on the tower of the fortress begins to strike.)
1
2
pp

L.
(in despair)
time, re_tard your flight, he will come! Be - lov - ed do not fail! Come,
3
4
5
6
pp
L.
come, for pity's sake, my hus - band, my only ref - uge!
7
8
9
ppp
poco
poco
10
11
cre - - - - - - - scen - - - - - do
12
f
dim.
pp
ppp
f

LISA
ff
A - las, 't is
ff
fff
Allegro giusto. (♩ = 120)
L.
true, then! With a murd' - rer's my
Allegro giusto.
sf
p
p
life is linked for ev - er - more! A murd' - rer
sf
has my soul in keep - - ing,
sf
p
sf
p
My In - no - cence none can re - store! His
sf

L.
guilt - y hand has forged my fet - ters, He
snared my hon - our with a lie, Yet both must
share one con - dem - na - - tion, to - geth - - er,
to - geth - - er, accurst by God we both must die! ac -
curst, we must die! Together and accurst, we
cre - - - - - scen -
do
cre - - scen - do

(Enter Herman)
L.
both must die!
(Wishes to fly)
'Tis
he! He comes! He is not guilty! He comes! My hours of grief are
Poco meno.
Poco meno.
espress.
o - ver, for once a - gain, dear, I am thine!
Go, fool-ish tears, and all re - pin - ing, For I am thine, as thou art
(Falls in his arms)
HERMAN.
(Kisses her)
mine! Be - lov - ed, I have come to thee!

Andante con moto. (♩=66)
LISA.
No sor - row or suf - f'ring can harm me, for
Andante con moto.
pp
L.
now thou art with me a - gain!
No
HERMAN.
Love, now I am with thee a - gain!
p
L.
more can life's ev - ils a - larm me.
Fare
H.
No more can life's e - vils a - larm me,
pp
pp
L.
well to our doubts and our pain!
No
H.
Fare - well to our doubts and our
mf

riten.
L.
sor_row or, suf - - f'ring can harm me, For now thou art with me a_
H.
pain! Our
riten.
p
Tempo I.
L.
gain! A
H.
tears and our ter_rors were on_ly a dream that has flown with the night!
Tempo I.
pp
p
L.
dream that has flown with the night! For_
H.
For - get thou wert trou_bled and lone - ly,
f
pp
L.
get thou wert trou_bled and lone - ly, And re_mem_ber our
H.
Once more I may clasp
pp
mf

L.
love and de - light, For - get thou wert trou-bled and lone - ly,
H.
thee! I may clasp thee! For - get thou wert sad and lone - ly,
L.
Our tears and ter-rors were on - ly Dreams that have flown with the night! Now a -
H.
Our tears and griefs were on - ly Dreams that have flown with the night! Now a -
riten.molto.
riten.molto.
f
mf
p
Andante.
Andantino. (♩ = 76)
L.
gain, thou art near me, My love!
H.
gain, I may clasp thee, My love!
Andante.
Andantino.
pp
mf
p
HERMAN.
Now sweet-heart mine, we
pp
pp

H.
must not lin - ger, the mo - ments fly... Come,
H.
are you read - y to go?
LISA.
I'll fol - low you,
L.
to earth's most dis - tant lim - its!
HERMAN.
Where shall we flee?
H.
a piacere
Ah where? The gaming house!

Moderato assai quasi andantino. (♩ = 84)

LISA.
O Heav'n! You must be raving, Herman!
HERMAN.
There lies a pile of glitt'ring
f
f
p
3
12
8
H
gold! to me, me a - lone, be - longs this wealth un
H.
told!
LISA.
O Her - man! Her - man! Why do you rave thus?
poco cre - scen - do mf
dim.
simile
L.
Re - mem - ber! Ah!
HERMAN.
I for - got, you do not know the
H.
se - cret! Three cards! I wan - ted... you re - mem - ber... long a -
poco cresc.
mf
cresc.

H.
go to make the Count - ess tell me!...
LISA.
O hor - ror!
mf
pesante
L.
This is mad - ness!
HERMAN.
From self - - ish fears,
H.
riten.
she kept her se-cret hid - den!
Lo stesso tempo. (♩ = ♩)
To - night. she, her-
Lo stesso tempo.
riten.
sfp
pp
H.
self came a-gain and named to me three cards, three
H.
cards!
LISA.
Ah! then 't was you who kill'd her?
HERMAN.
O,
mp

H.
No! Why should I? I on - ly showed her the
pp
(he laughs)
H.
pis - tol, And sud - den_ly the queer old witch fell back_ward!
cresc.
f
LISA.
Moderato mosso. (♩ = 104)
Then all is true then! Too true!
Moderato mosso.
p
f
L.
ff
A_las,'tis
ff
fff

Allegro giusto. (♩ = 120)
true, then, with a mur - d'rer's my
Allegro giusto. Yes! Yes! I tell you,
life is linked for ev - er - more! A mur-d'rer
I hold her se - - cret fast!
has my soul in his keep - - ing,
'Twas by my hand she died. Three cards,
My in - no - cence none can re - store! His
three cards she named to me at last!

L.
guilt - y hand has forged my fet - ters, He
H.
'Twas fate that will'd this crime should be, 'Twas
sf p
p
L.
snared my hon - our with a lie,
H.
fate de - creed I should do mur - der,
sf p
p
L.
Yet both must share one con - dem - na - tion,
H.
O won in such a fat al way!
ff
sf p
p
L.
To - geth - er, to - geth - er
H.
Three cards, three cards!
p cre - scen - do

L.
ac_curst by God, we both must die! Ac
H.
Yes, fate de_creed I should do
f
pp
L.
curst we must die!
H.
mur_der. O won in such a fat_al
cre - - - -
scen - - - do
L
Più Allegro.
To_gether, and ac_curst, we both must die! Ah no!
H.
way! For my three cards the price I pay!
f
f
Più Allegro.
sf
p
p
L.
It can_not be! You rave, poor Her_man!
fp
p

HERMAN (beside himself).
Yes I, that third man im_pell'd by des_pair, Who
cre scen do
H.
strove from the Count_ess her se_cret to tear_ the three, the sev_en, the
f p
sfp
LISA.
L.
Be what you may, I'll still be true to you! Es_cape and
H.
ace!
pp
p sfp
HERMAN.
L.
come with me, I'll save you yet! Hah! she told me, She, her_
cre scen do
H.
self, re_vealed them: the three, the sev_en, the ace!
f p
sfp p sfp

End of 6th Scene.

SCENE VII.

№ 22. Chorus and scene.

While it lasts, our cares we'll bur - y,
While it lasts, our cares we'll bur - y,
Age we can - not long a - void, While youth lasts our
Age we can - not long a - void,
Pass the wine, pass the wine!
cares we'll bur - y,
Age we can - not long a - void,
Now pass the wine, and let's make mer - ry,
Youth should be en - joy'd!
Age we can - not long a -

void,
Let youth be en_joy'd!
mf
Deal the cards and
p
pass the gob - - let, Let us float on pleasure's stream!
mf
Deal the cards and pass the gob - - let, Let us float on pleasure's
p
mf
p
stream!
Stake your mon - - ey, friends, and double it,
mf

Life is pas-sing like a dream! Deal the cards and pass the gob - - let, Let us float on pleasure's stream!
Deal the cards and pass the gob - let, Let us float on pleasure's
Stake your mon - - ey, friends, and doub-le it, Life is
stream, for life pas - - ses like a dream, for life
cresc.
pas-sing like a dream! Life's pas-sing like a dream
pas-ses like a dream! pas-sing like a dream

ff
Pass the wine, and let's be
ff
Pass the wine, and let's be mer - ry!
ff
mer - ry!
Youth was meant to be en - joy'd!
Youth was meant to be en - joy'd!
While it lasts, our cares we'll bur - y,
While it lasts, our cares we'll bur - y,
Age we can - not long a - void, age we can - - not
Age we can - not long a - void, age we can - - not

Deal the cards, pass the wine!
long a_void! Youth was meant to be en_joy'd!
long a_void! Now pass the wine and let's make mer - ry
Youth should be en - - joy'd! Age we can_not long a -
void! Let youth be en - joy'd!
Sostenuto. (ma lo stesso tempo.)
TCHAPLITSKY.
I pass pa_ro_li!
SOURIN.
NARUMOV.
My gain!... I
Sostenuto. (ma lo stesso tempo.)
p

TCHEKALINSKY (shuffling).
Tchapl.
Pa_ro_li_pe! Now, who will stake?
N.
trump it!
At_ten_dez!
SOURIN
Tchek.
Ace! That's Mi_ran_do_le.
TOMSKY (to the Prince).
What are you do_ing
mf
p
T.
here? I nev_er once have seen you here at play be_
THE PRINCE.
T.
fore. True! This is my first vis_it. The pro_verb you
mf

P.
know it: „un-luck-y in love, luck - y at cards"...
p
p
TOMSKY.
What do you mean to say?
THE PRINCE.
That I'm no lon-ger en-
P.
gaged. But do not ask me more! The wound is
mf
P.
smart-ing still! Revenge has brought me here! You
f
p

P.
know the pro-verb: „luck - y in love, un - luck - - - y at
cre - - scen - - do
Tempo come prima.
TOMSKY.
Tell me, what is your meaning?
P.
cards!“ Wait and see!
CHORUS.
ff
Pass the wine and let's be
ff
Pass the wine and let's be mer - ry
Tempo come prima.
ff
mer - ry, Youth is meant to be en - joy'd!
Youth is meant to be en - joy'd!

While it lasts, our cares we'll bur - y,
While it lasts, our cares we'll bur - y,
Age we can - not long a - void, While youth lasts, our
Age we can - not long a - void, While youth lasts, our
cares we'll bury,
Deal the cards, pass the wine,
Age we can - not long a - void,
cares we'll bury,
Now pass the wine and let's be mer - ry,
Youth should be en - joy'd!
Age we can - not long a -

(The players join those at the supper table.)
void,
Let youth be en - joy'd!
Sostenuto. (ma lo stesso tempo.)
TCHEKALINSKY
Come, gent_le_men, let Tomsky sing a jov - ial dit - ty!
Sostenuto. (ma lo stesso tempo.)
p
poco cre - scen - do
CHORUS.
Sing, Toms - ky, sing, but let it be a jol - - ly song,
Sing, Toms - ky, sing, but let it be a
mf
TOMSKY.
I am not in the mood.
TCHEK.
Hey! What's a -
A song of love and wine!
jol_ly song, a song!
p

Tchek
miss my friend? drink deep, then you'll feel bet - ter! Now, friends, lets
Tchek.
drink to Toms - ky's health! Hur - rah!
CHORUS.
Here, Toms - ky, here's to you, Hur - rah!
cre - scen - do
hur - rah! hur - rah!
Hur - rah! hur - rah! hur - rah!
hur - rah! hur - rah!

№ 23. Tomsky's Song and Chorus of Gamblers.

Text by Derjavin.
Andante. (♩= 76)
TOMSKY.
Andante.
PIANO.
Adagio. (♩= 58)
Adagio.
If all girls with wings were fit - ted, If o'er hill and dale they
flit - ted, Perch - ing on the trees to rest,
I would be a branch well - lad - en, Shelt' - ring man - y a sweet
maid - en, By at least a thou - sand blest, By at least a thou - sand

Andante.
Adagio.
T.
blest!
There they'd
CHORUS.
Bra_vo!
Bra_vo!
O sing an_oth_er verse!
Andante.
Adagio.
sit and sing while rest_ing, In the spring be bu_sy nest_ing, Rear their Young and cal_low
brood!
Then re_nounc_ing wine and play_ing, By my
song-birds al_ways staying, I might be for ev_er good, I might be for ev_er

Andante.
T.
good!
CHORUS.
Bra - vo! Bra - vo! That's a fam - ous song, it's
Andante.
splen - did! Bra - vo! Tomsky, thanks! Then re - nounc - ing wine and
playing, By my song - birds al - ways stay - ing, I might be for ev - er
scen do
good, I might be for ev - er - good!

TCHEKALINSKY.
Meno.
Well now, friends, in our good old style we'll sing the gambler's song!
Meno.
mf
f
ff
Allegro molto vivo. (♩ = 160)
p
TCHEK.
TCHAP.
Let it rain, let it sleet, Round the ta-bles we'll meet, dai - ly!
NARUM.
SOURIN.
p
f
CHORUS.
Let it rain, let it sleet, Round the ta-bles we'll meet, dai - ly!
p
f

Tchek.
Tchap.
There our hundreds we stake, And our loss - es we take, gai - - ly!
N.
S.
p
f
CHOR.
There our hun - dreds we stake, And our loss - es we take, gai - - ly!
p
f
Tchek.
Tchap.
All our gains we chalk up, While we pass round the cup, mad - - ly!
N.
S.
p
f
CHOR.
All our gains we chalk up, While we pass round the cup, mad - - ly!
p
f

Tchek.
Tchap.
Till the dawn is a - glow, And we rise up to go, sad - ly!
N.
S.
mf
CHOR.
Till the dawn is a - glow, And we rise up to go, sad - ly!
ff
mf
Tchek.
Tchap.
ff
Let it rain, let it sleet, round the ta - bles we'll meet, dai - - ly,
N.
S.
ff
ff
mf
ff
CHOR.
Let it rain, let it sleet, round the ta - bles we'll meet dai - - ly,
ff
mf
ff

Tchek.
Tchap.
All our gains we chalk up, While we pass round the cup,
N.
S.
sempre ff
mad - ly! Till the dawn is a-glow and we
rise up to go, sad - ly! mad - ly, sad - ly!

Tchek.
Tchap.
mad - ly! There our hun - dreds we stake, and our loss - es we
N.
S.
mad - ly! There our hun - dreds we stake, and our loss - es we
take, and our loss - es we take, gai - ly,
take, and our loss - es we take, gai - ly,
(Whistles, cries and dancing.)
dai - ly, gai - ly, dai - ly, gai - ly!
dai - ly, gai - ly, dai - ly, gai - ly!
8

№ 24. Closing scene.

TCHAPLITSKY.
A - gainst you!
SOURIN.
Then I will back the ta - ble...
mf
p
TCHAPLITSKY.
I win!
NAROUMOV.
Now trans - port to the ten!
(Enter Herman.)
sf p
sfp
PRINCE (catching sight of him.)
So, my pre - sent - i - ment was right on this oc -
mf
P.
ca - sion!
(To Tomsky)
Per - haps I may have need of you as se - cond,
p
p

TOMSKY.
P.
Tomsky; I think you'll see me through?
You can re-ly on
T.
me!
CHORUS.
What! Her-man, you!
How late you are!
What! Her-man, Where were you? How
TCHEKALINSKY.
Come, sit by me, per-haps you'll bring me luck.
Where were you?
late you are!

L'istesso tempo.
SOURIN.
ritenuto
Where have you been? Where then? To hell and back,eh? You look uncommon
Andante moderato. (♩ = 80)
TCHEK.
S.
queer! As pa_le as any ghost! Have you been ill?
Andante moderato.
p marcato
(Tchekalinsky acquiesces with a silent bow.)
HERMAN. Recit.
SOURIN.
I want to take a hand at cards. What next, what next! Our Her_man
CHORUS.
What next, what
S.
playing!
NAROUMOV. Recit.
Dear fellow, good
next! Our Her_man turn_ing gamb_ler! Her - man!
(Herman takes a card and covers it with a bank note.)
What next, our Her - man turn_ing gambler! Her_man, Her_man!
colla parte

a tempo
TCHEK.
luck! You've watched us long with hung-ry eyes! Your
a tempo
marcato
p
Tchek.
HERMAN.
stakes? For-ty thousand!
CHORUS.
For - ty
For - ty thou-sand!
For-ty thou-sand!
SOURIN.
Recit.
Have you discovered the three cards of the Countess?
Forty thousand! What a stake!
thousand! Her-man, are you mad?
I think you must be mad!
colla parte
f
ff

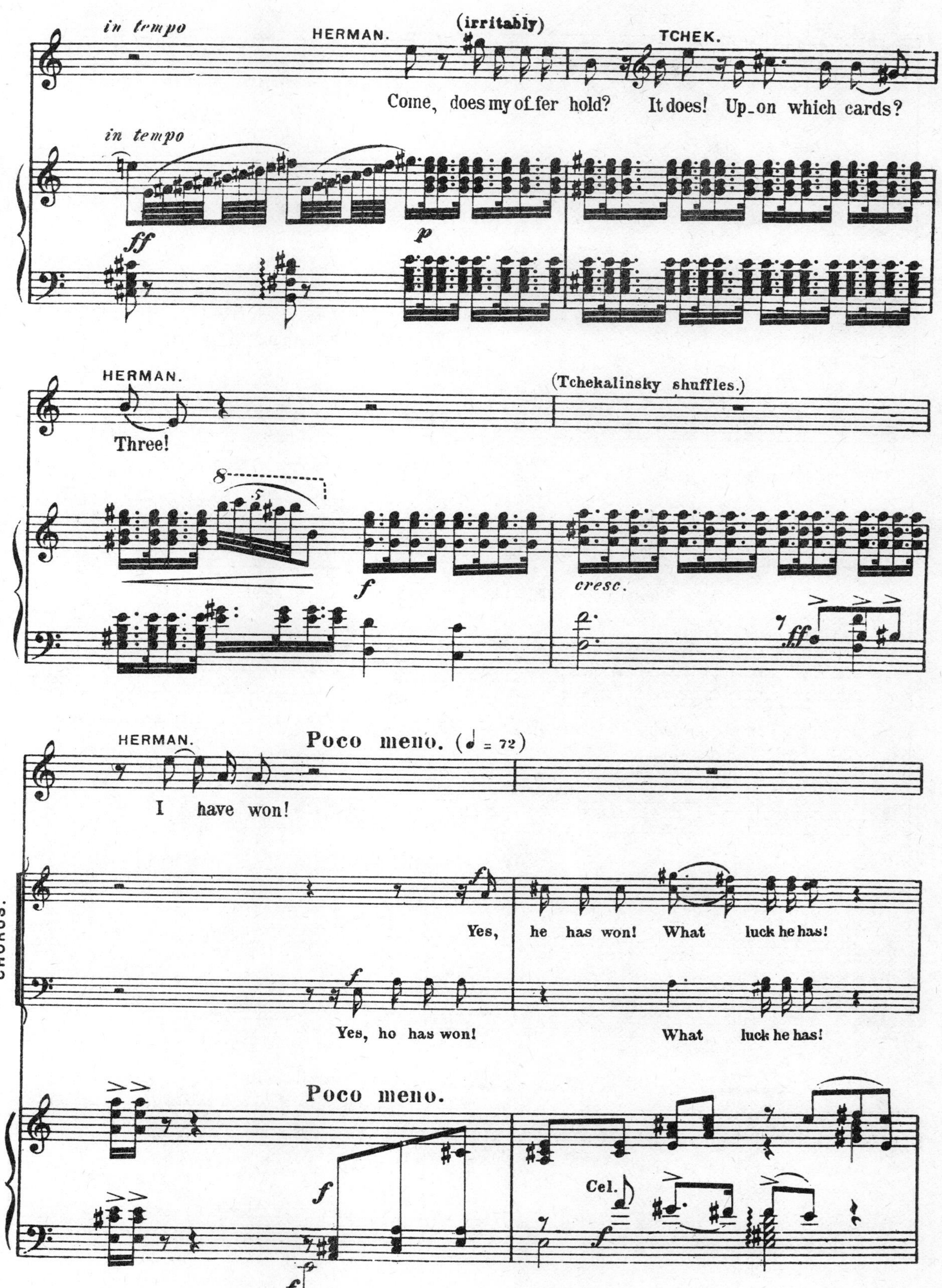
in tempo
HERMAN.
(irritably)
Come, does my of_fer hold?
TCHEK.
It does! Up_on which cards?
in tempo
ff
p
HERMAN.
Three!
(Tchekalinsky shuffles.)
f
cresc.
ff
HERMAN.
Poco meno. (♩ = 72)
I have won!
CHORUS.
Yes, he has won! What luck he has!
Yes, ho has won! What luck he has!
Poco meno.
f
Cel.
f
f

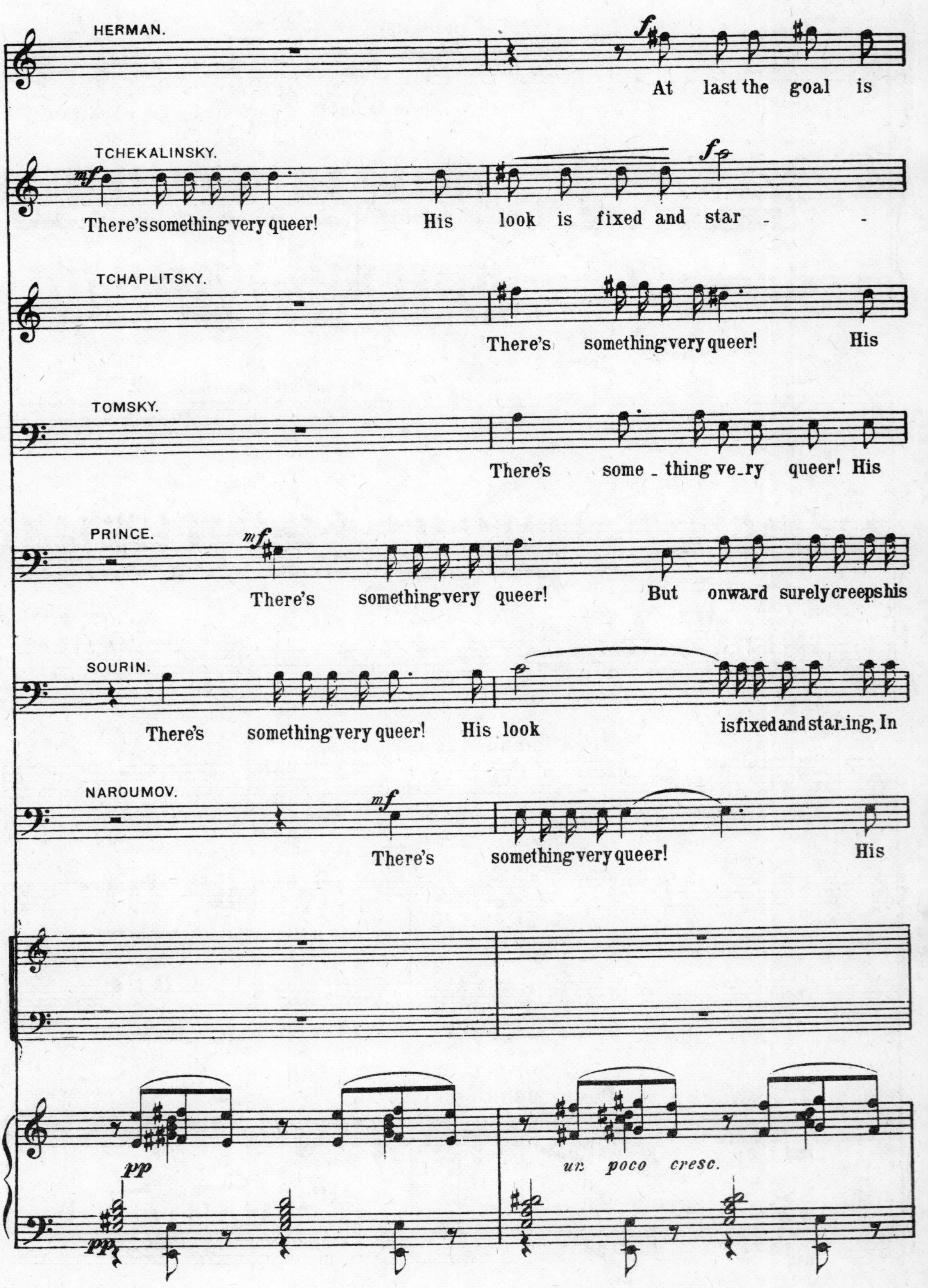
HERMAN.
f
At last the goal is
TCHEKALINSKY.
mf
There's something very queer! His look is fixed and star -
f
TCHAPLITSKY.
There's something very queer! His
TOMSKY.
There's some _ thing ve_ry queer! His
PRINCE.
mf
There's something very queer! But onward surely creeps his
SOURIN.
There's something very queer! His look is fixed and star_ing, In
NAROUMOV.
mf
There's something very queer! His
pp
un poco cresc.
pp

H.
reached, All goes with_out a hitch. No!
Tchek.
mf
ing, In me he rous - es fear, There's mad - ness in his dar - ing!
Tchap.
look is fixed and star_ing. In me he rouses fear! There's
T.
look, his look, is fixed and star_ing, There's mad - ness in his dar_ing,
P.
hour! Now my re_venge draws near,
S.
me he rouses fear, There's madness, madness in his dar - ing! Yes,
N.
look is fixed and star_ing, In me he rous - es fear, In me he rouses fear!

H.
No! she's not failed me, aft - er all, the strange old
Tchek.
dim.
Yes, there's something ver-y queer! There's mad - - ness in his
Tchap.
dim.
madness in his dar - ing! Yes, there's something ver-y queer! His look is
T.
dim.
In me he rous-es fear! Yes, There's something very strange and
P.
dim.
Now my re - venge draws near, I have him in my
S.
dim.
There's something ver - y queer! See, his look is fixed and staring. In
N.
dim.
Yes! There's something ver-y queer! There's mad-ness in his dar-ing, In
mf
dim.

H.
Un poco riten.
witch!
Tchek.
p
dar-ing! In me he rouses fear!
Tchap.
Un poco riten.
p
fixed and star-ing! In me he rouses fear!
T.
p
queer!
P.
p
Un poco riten.
pow'r Now my re-venge draws near!
S.
p
me he rous-es fear!
N.
p
me he rous-es fear!
mf
Un poco riten.
dim.
There's something ver-y queer! His look is fixed and star-ing, In me he rous-es fear,
mf
dim.
Un poco riten.
p
dim.

Tempo I (♩= 80)
TCHEKALINSKY.
Your winnings! Take them up!
HERMAN.
No! Double or
ppp
There's mad-ness in his dar-ing!
ppp
Tempo I.
pp
p
marcato
p
H.
quits!
O, he is rav-ing, poor old Her-man! Come, Tche-kal-
O, he is rav-ing, poor old Her-man! Come, Tche-kal-in-sky, leave off
in-sky, leave off play-ing, He looks so strange and
play-ing, leave off play-ing, He looks so strange and
mf

HERMAN.
You play?
Here! The seven!
TCHEKALINSKY.
I do! What cards?
(Shuffles.)
wild!
H.
I win!
He wins a_gain!
H.
Well, you are look_ing down cast!
Why surely, all is not right, he's cheat_ing!

(Laughs hysterically.)
H.
You're ner vous? You fear me?
Bring wine, bring wine!
CHORUS.
Her - - man,
What ails you?
(With glass in hand.)
Moderato con moto. (♩=100.)
What is our life?
A game!
Aye, right and wrong are
Moderato con moto.
emp - ty dreams!
And work and hon - our just a

H.
riten.
name! Now say, who's hap_pier of us two?
mf
riten.
p
Un poco meno animato.
Tempo I.
To day 't is I, To morrow you! For scruples do not
Un poco meno animato.
Tempo I.
p
f
wait, But catch your luck and use it! Let them re_pine who lose it,
mf
f
ad libitum.
a tempo
Let them re_pine who lose it, And curse, and curse their
sf
p
f
p

Tempo I.
H.
sor - - - - ry fate! What's certain? Death
Tempo I.
stringendo
mf
f
ff
p
a_lone! When o'er life's sea our course we
f
p
take, Death is the one sure port we
make. And which of us has Death in view?
riten.
mf
riten.
p

Un poco meno animato.
Tempo I.
H.
To day 'tis me, To_morrow you! For scruples do not wait, But
Un poco meno animato.
Tempo I.
p
catch your luck and use it! Let them re_pine who lose it,
mf
f
sf
ff
Let them re_pine who lose it, And curse their
ff
Allegro.
sor - - - - - ry fate!
stringendo
Allegro.
p
f
ff

Allegro giusto. (♩= 120)
TCHEKALINSKY.
H.
You'll stake once more!
No, take your gains!
I think you
Allegro giusto.
(Tchekalinsky lays the money on the table.)
HERMAN.
Tchek.
have the dev - il's luck at cards!
And if I have, what
H.
then?
What does it mat - ter!
Who
H.
feels disposed now,
To stake the lot up

THE PRINCE (stepping forward).
H.
dis
Fürst.
on one card? Well?
I will!
CHORUS.
Prince,
Prince, come a - way!
come a - way! Do not stake, For this is not fair
Do not stake, For this is not fair play, not fair
THE PRINCE.
ad libitum
I know what I am doing; friends! We
play, but mad - ness! Don't stake!
play, but mad - ness! Dont stake!

HERMAN (agitated).
have old scores to set_tle!
You!
You, a_gainst me?
a tempo
THE PRINCE.
I!
Come, shuf_fle,
Tche_kal_in_sky!
(Tchekalinsky shuffles.)
cresc.
HERMAN (uncovers a card).
My
ace!
ad libitum
THE PRINCE.
No!
'T is
your
Queen
of

Moderato assai. (♩= 92)
HERMAN.
riten.
THE PRINCE.
P.
Spades! What! Queen of Spades? There, in your hand, you hold the Queen of
Moderato assai.
riten.
p
Andante non troppo. (Come prima.)
(The Ghost of the Countess appears. Everybody retreats before Herman.)
HERMAN (in terror)
P.
Spades! The Count_ess! You! And here! What bodes your
Andante non troppo. (Come prima.)
pp
un poco marcato ma sempre pp
H.
laugh_ter? To shame and mad_ness you have brought me! Ac_
H.
curs_ _ed witch! What? What do you want of me?

H.
Speak! Hah! my life? Well take it, then, my
(He stabs himself. The ghost vanishes. Some of the guests bend over Herman, who has fallen to the ground.)
Moderato mosso e agitato.
H.
life is yours!
CHORUS.
Poor Her_man!
Poor Her_man! What a
cresc.
Moderato mosso e agitato.
What a dread _ _ ful, un _ hal _ low'd end is his! He
dread _ ful, un_hal_low'd end is his! He lives, he
cresc.

(Herman comes to himself, and seeing the Prince, tries to raise himself up)
lives, he breathes!
lives, he breathes!
f
dim.
HERMAN.
Prince! Prince, for -
p
Ritenuto.
H.
ad libitum
give, for-give! All's ov - er... ov - er... I am dy - ing...
Ritenuto.
Andante.

Andantino. (♩ = 84)
H
Who is this? Li - sa? You here? God a - bove!
Andantino.
pp
pp espress.
H.
For what? For what? You for - give me? Yes?
p
H.
Curse me not! Ah! How I have loved you, Li - sa!
cre - scen - do
mf
dim.
(He dies.)
H.
An - gel, con - demn me not! Belov - ed! Ah!
riten.
p
mf
p
pp
morendo

End of the Opera.